I0114191

ISLE OF THE AMAZONS IN THE VERMILION SEA

ISLE OF THE AMAZONS IN THE VERMILION SEA

compiled and narrated by

GREGORY MACDONALD

illustrated by

JUDITH PALMER

39 WEST PRESS

39 WEST PRESS
Kansas City, MO
www.39WestPress.com

39 WEST
PRESS

First Edition: April 2019

ISBN: 978-1-946358-14-1

Library of Congress Control Number: 2019930908

10 9 8 7 6 5 4 3 2 1

Interior Illustrations: Judith Palmer
Book Design: j.d.tulloch

39WP-26

For Mat, in loving memory.

CONTENTS

Know thee that at the right hand of the Indies there is an island named California, very close to that part of the Terrestrial Paradise, which was Inhabited by black women, without a single man among them, and that They lived in the manner of Amazons. They were robust of body, with strong and passionate hearts. The island itself is one of the wildest in the world on account of the bold and craggy rocks. Their weapons were all made of gold ... The island everywhere abounds with gold and precious stones, and upon It no other metal was found ... They had many ships with which they sailed to other coasts to make forays, and the men whom they took as prisoners they killed ... In this island there are many griffins ... [And] there ruled over that island of California a queen of majestic proportions, more beautiful than all the others, and in the very vigor of her womanhood ...

–Vasco de Lobeira (circa 1400)

MAP: Gregory MacDonald, 2005
(Not to Scale)

INTRODUCTION

California. It is only fitting that the name given this paradoxical "island"—forbidding yet so alluring—was a product of antiquated romantic fiction, half-way around the known world at the time.

In the late 1400s, Spanish literary romanticist Garci Rodríguez de Montalvo wrote an epic 1800-page chivalric romance entitled *Amadis de Gaula*. In the fifth and final volume of the work, concerning the brave knight Explandián, Montalvo described an island "at the right hand of the Indies" that he named California. This island was ruled by the giant Queen Calafía whose subjects were robust, black Amazon women. It was a land of ferocious griffins, of gold and precious stones, "made up of the wildest cliffs and the sharpest precipices found anywhere in the world."

Although the island had been conceived in fiction, it was too enticing to remain a myth. Spanish nobility, royalty, conquerors, and explorers from Columbus to Cortés seemed powerless to resist its spell, pushing ever onward in search of the fabled isle "on the right hand of the Indies." When the latter was given command of a later expedition to Mexico (after his conquest of the Aztec empire), he was also charged with finding the mystical island. "Explore. Find gold. Find the island of Queen Calafía," ordered King Charles V. As fortune would have it, Cortés learned of just such a place where dark women, pearls, and gold could be found in the then-perceived vicinity of the Indies.

In 1535, Cortés landed at Santa Cruz, on the Bay of La Paz, not to find an earthly paradise inhabited by sirens but, instead, a desolate land and a hostile assemblage of unwashed indigenes. The first settlement of California was a dismal failure. Cortés had conquered the Land of the Aztecs but the Land of the Amazons had conquered Cortés. The name California stuck, ironically, as if to ridicule the once mighty *conquistador*.

But the myth endured. The "island" was determined to be a peninsula then wished back into being an island by explorers several times over. It wasn't until 1701, that Padre Eusebio Kino, from atop Mt. Hornaday in the Sonoran desert, sighted the terminus of the Gulf and the uninterrupted peninsula farther west.

It is surprising, therefore, that with later exploration, Montalvo's description was, in many ways, a fitting one. Granted, there were no Amazon women or soaring griffins, but there were pearls in abundance. And the fearsome *Sierra de la Giganta* mountains were made up of wild cliffs and sharp precipices ... And who is the *Giganta* for whom the range is named? Why, Queen Calafía of course! Montalvo had indeed set the stage.

In this anthology I have assembled descriptions of Baja, California and the Sea of Cortez from the mid-sixteenth century to the present. Some of these could be classified as being in the passive vein—impressions and observations—while others are clearly action-generated. Still others, which are my favorites, are products of intense passion for the region—from those who have felt its touch and have become part of its land and sea. There are well-known authors represented here—Steinbeck, Gardner, Cannon, Crosby—but mostly there are those who simply have been moved to record their personal impressions and experiences.

Choosing nuggets from nearly five hundred years of recorded history and narrative expression was a delightful endeavor. These came in many forms: diaries, logbooks, letters, field notes, books, periodicals, guest books, journals, and works of poetry. I favored the simplest and shortest impressions and descriptions because they seemed to say it best.

The reader will notice that I have grouped quotations into subject matter instead of strict chronology. This resulted in some remarkably similar experiences that were sometimes a hundred or more years apart; only the dates reveal this.

I must be one of the aforementioned individuals who has become a part of the Baja Experience, because so much of what follows on these pages touched my entire field of emotions and all my senses. The thrill of Arthur North's overland adventures, the tenderness of his daughter's observations of nature, the splendor of a Griffing Bancroft sunrise, the horror of Scammon's whaling enterprises, the humor of Miller's *Cruise of the Cow* ... these and so much more went into the mix.

Research for this anthology easily could have been limited to visiting libraries, used book stores, historical societies—or referring to my own Collection on Baja. Perhaps it was merely an excuse to go there, but I chose, in addition, to visit most of the settings that inspired the descriptions contained herein. Retracing old routes and searching for time-forgotten places and relics led to many unexpected adventures of my own.

My partner in this undertaking has been artist Judith Palmer. She has won many awards, and her work is housed in collections in the United States and abroad. As enthusiastic as she is talented, Judith has been a joy to work with. She is also a person who knows Baja and therefore was able to capture its essence in expressive line drawings. Her husband, Ben Stoltzfus, an author and Professor Emeritus in literature and creative writing from UC Riverside, edited the text and is also a contributor. Ben has had a beach-front *casita* in the East Cape area for several decades and relishes every opportunity to go to Baja.

We hope that you enjoy your visit to this magical land and sea.

–Riverside, California (August 2014)

FOREWORD

LOWER CALIFORNIA

From Its Mythical Past to the Present
The Land • The Sea • The People

It is bewildering to see descriptions of the land change from a God-forsaken "thorny heap of rocks" in the seventeenth century to a miraculous and alluring wonderland in the Twentieth and Twenty-first centuries. In between the history of the region is an entirely disjointed one. As Bruce Berger put it, "... cultures that have no more in common but that they played out their lives on the same platform."

It is clear that the fascination with Baja in current times is that, being a remote and therefore forgotten appurtenance of Mexico and California, it was spared the ravages of what we have come to term "progress" in the United States. Try to imagine a greater contrast than that of the mostly-primitive Baja peninsula with the world's most advanced civilization, one step north across an imaginary border line. But this is changing fast, north and south, day by day. Reason enough to collect a few snapshots of a previously unspoiled land.

As for the Sea of Cortez, it was surprising to me that early explorers and missionaries were neither impressed nor inspired by a sea that was later to be described by Jacques Cousteau as "the World Aquarium." Early references are limited to harrowing tales of survival in a tempest's rage—the jettisoning of livestock and precious cargo to remain afloat—or desperately trying to find landfall even if it meant limping back to the mainland. As you will read, those intrepid souls were consumed by coping with nature, not worshiping it. And so it was for several hundred years. In fact, it wasn't until well into the twentieth century that there was an awakening to the splendor and wonder of the Sea of Cortez. Therefore, in collecting memorable descriptions, I have concentrated on the current and timely. But this is a sad irony, because the best descriptions are coming at the very close of the Sea of Cortez's five-million-year virgin run.

After encountering the Amazons and their mythical past, the Jesuits and their lowly converts, our journey begins at Land's End, the southern tip of Baja, and moves north by land and sea, over mountains, across deserts, and through valleys toward oases, towns, and bays until we reach San Felipe. Finally, we arrive at the mouth of the Colorado River where it once emptied its abundant waters into the Gulf.

ISLE OF THE AMAZONS IN THE VERMILION SEA

A BROKEN LADDER

It's difficult to climb Baja California's ladder of history;
Blame it on so many gaps between the rungs.

Setting the stage was an advanced race of aborigines;
Tall and robed, they chronicled life with fine rock murals,
Then vanished without trace.

AN EMPTY LAND
Next, in a curious case of de-evolution, arrived a lowly lot.
Near stone-age, they were content to grub and gather.
In came the Black Robes to save their happy souls,
Exterminating them in the process with foreign microbes.
Then Royal expulsion was the Jesuit reward.

AN EMPTY LAND
Enter the Californios, remote frontiersmen of valley and shore,
Their unshared stories evaporated in the desert air.

Now arrives an imported populace, eyes forward, no glint of the past.

–Gregory MacDonald (2012)

Palmer

Baja California is a fierce, sun-blasted strip of desert roughly 800 miles long that separated itself from the Mexican mainland in a slow tectonic slide about five million years ago. The Pacific Ocean rushed in to fill the void, forming the Gulf of California, the youngest of the world's deep-water gulfs. This vast arm of the Pacific, two miles deep at its mouth, was once known as the Vermilion Sea, and indeed, under a rising sun, the warm, tranquil water shimmers like pale blood.

The mountains are stark, ridged and crenellated and bare. The land supports a variety of obdurate and malicious flora: there are thistles underfoot and cardón cacti towering overhead. It is little given to agriculture or ranching. Every growing thing, or so it seems, sticks, stabs, or stinks.

–Tim Cahill (1993)

22nd. Under way at 6. Found the trail. What a cursed country! Rocks, thorns and this cursed cactus! The devil's own plant. Old Joe, confound him, got up several estampedes. Plenty of water but little grass. Nye shot a huge rattlesnake. We are hard up but full of spirit. My only pair of breaches is in rags, used up by the thorns. Well, my skin is sound yet. The only vegetation was cactus of every size, shape, and form. It frequently formed a barrier through which we were obliged to force our horses, the sharp points piercing us and them. The ground everywhere was literally covered with thorny plants, indeed the region seems to have been gotten up in a spirit of malediction.

23rd. Another day of toil and vexation. Had a two hour's hunt for a horse this morning ... These stones in the trail look like pieces of junk bottles. They are obsidian and cut like knives. The poor unshod horses leave blood at every track ...

–W. C. S. Smith (1849)

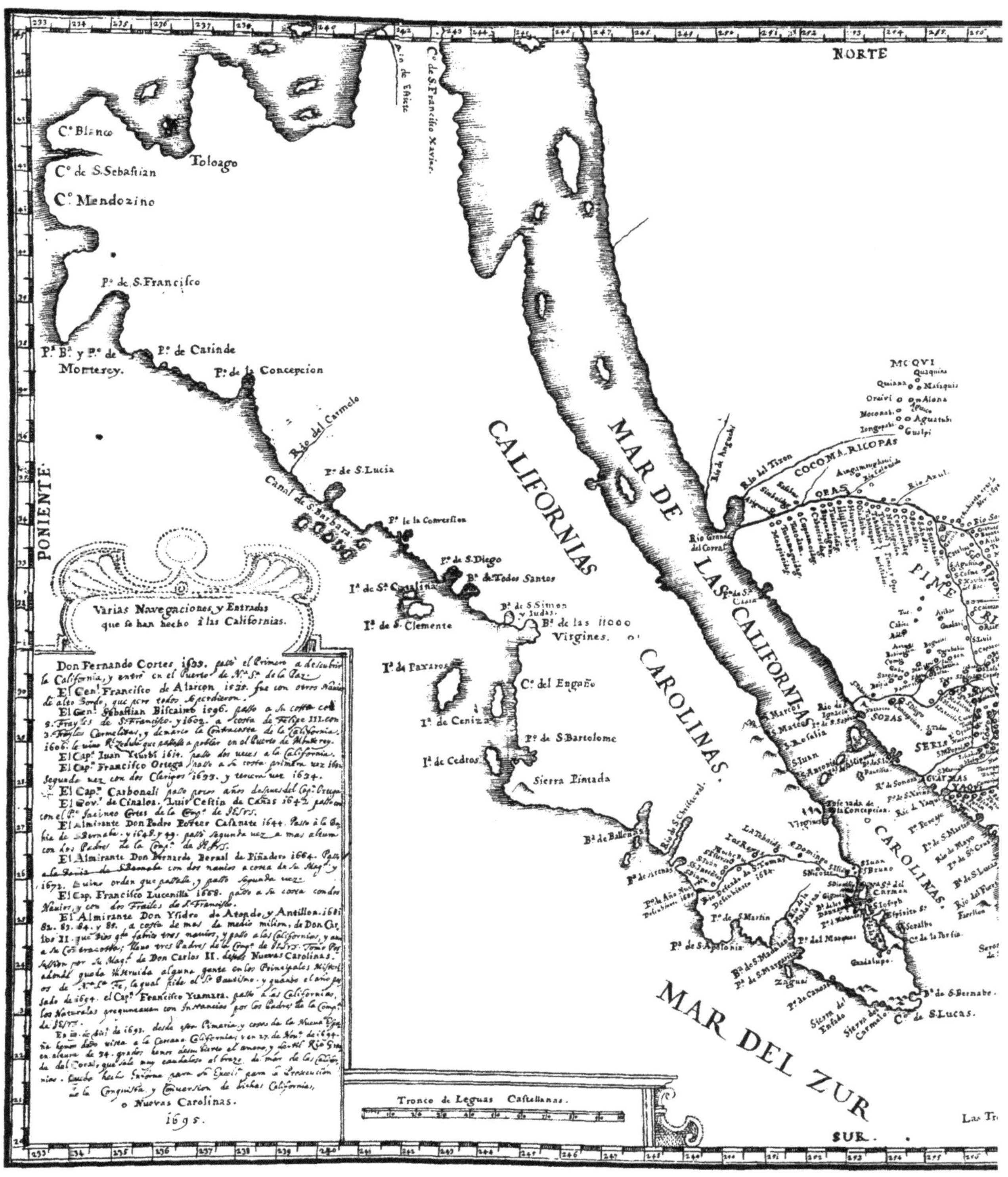

Kino's *Teatro de los Trabajos Apostólicos.* Drawn in 1695–1696

(From the original manuscript)

Far to the Northwest of the main route of the conquistadors, twice found and twice forgotten, the Gulf of California is the heart of one of the wildest and richest regions in the whole span of Spanish Glory. Geographically this region touches two totally different civilizations—that of our own southwest and that of Mexico proper—but in reality it hangs in space between them, its resources utilized by neither, its history neglected by both, its strange, fierce life altogether its own.

–Randolph Leigh (1940)

California, as the main section lying near the Tropic of Cancer is called Antonomasia, stretches north from its tip in the form of a half-moon for more than five hundred leagues, although it is not definitely known whether it ultimately adjoins the mainland on the north, or whether, as in all probability a fact, it is an island; on these points, however, writers do not agree. With a varying width of twenty, thirty, forty, and fifty leagues, it is covered mainly with mountains, precipices, and valleys.

While there is some land available for planting at almost all the missions, yet at many of these it has become necessary to transport and at time drag supplies over mountains which, generally speaking, are thickly covered with boulders.

–Father Sigismundo Taraval (1734)

How it happened that the aborigines of the peninsula had remained at a level of culture almost as low as that found anywhere on earth, while to the west and to the south the great pre-Columbian civilization rose to heights which still astonish our archeologists; no one can say ... [Clavigero] declared that when the missionaries first arrived in Baja "not a hut, nor an earthen jar, not an instrument of metal nor a piece of cloth" was to be found." They lived principally on what they could pick up—locusts, lizards, caterpillars, spiders, and lice from their hair, plus cactus fruits in season ... Usually starving, though occasionally gorged, they followed vultures to rob them of their prey.

–Joseph Wood Krutch (1961)

From thence [Azatlán] ten dayes further I shall goe to find the Amazons, which some say dwell in the Sea, some in an arme of the Sea, and that they are rich, and accounted of the people for Goddesses, and whiter than other women. They use Bowes, Arrows, and Targets; have many and great townes; at a certain time [they] admit them [men] to accompanie them, which bring up the males as these the female issue.

–Nuño de Guzmán (1530)

From the fourth *Carta de Relacion* to the king of Spain:

... and likewise there was brought to me a story from the lords of the province Cihualtán who made strong assertions about an island that was entirely populated by women, without any male and that certain times men who had access to them go from terra firma ... and if they bear women, they keep them; and if men, they get rid of them; and that this island is ten days journey from this province; and that it is rich in pearls and gold. I will labor at making preparations to learn the truth and will write at length about it to your majesty.

–Hernán Cortés (1524)

It is inhabited by bestial, naked, people. Virgins went naked, women were presented a blanket only when married.

–Pedro de Castaneda (1540)

... It can clearly be seen that this account mingles, as in all legends, truth with fantasy, since all about the gold and women alone is immediately obvious as fiction; but as to pearls, which were a much coveted reality in the northwestern peninsula of Mexico, one cannot help but think that the island referred to in the reports carried to Cortez from Colina was without the slightest doubt, Lower California.

–Pablo Martinez (1956)

What is [lower] California? From the top to the bottom and from one side to another it is nothing but a thorny heap of stones, or paths, waterless rock rising between two oceans; consequently, as one might expect, it is desolate and almost without inhabitants. I often say in jest: either California is without exception the most miserable country under the sun, or if an equally miserable or worse country was ever discovered by the Argonauts then California was the model for making it .. To put it briefly—heaven is, as it were, closed against California.

It is possibly true, as I have often read and heard about other savage peoples, that this handful of black unwashed people are human in nothing but shape and mind, or rather, that the only thing that distinguishes them from the animals is that they have no horns. For I have seen most of them going about naked and they still nearly all do. They live in the open air; daily out to pasture; never wash unless with urine; when they drink they lie down flat, put their heads in the water and lap it up like cows.

–Jacob Baegert (1752)

A land the most unfortunate, ungrateful, and miserable of the world.

–Padre Miguel Venegas (1739)

Nothing but rocks, cliffs, declivitious mountains and measureless sandy wastes, broken only by impassable walls.

–Wenceslaus Linck (1766)

The [mid-18th century] natives of Baja California were at a primitive cultural level, for they lived solely by hunting, fishing, and seed gathering and had neither letters, agriculture, nor architecture. Anthropologists called such people lower nomads—or marginal peoples. They were forced by circumstance to roam about within restricted areas to obtain food.

Their menu included such things as roots, grasses, and seeds, birds, horses, burros, mules, dogs, cats, rats, mice, snakes, and bats; walnut leaves, and certain types of edible wood; leather cured and uncured; the bones of birds, sheep, goats and calves. Fish and meat already putrid were eaten without discrimination.

–Msgr. Francis J. Weber (1984)

They do truly strange things at their meals. At the time of the gathering of the Pitaja they eat until they are satisfied; but in order to make use of them again after having eaten and digested them, they do not put aside their deposits. With inexpressible patience, from what was previously pitaja, they separate the very tiny seeds of the fruit which remain; they toast them, grind them, and keep them thus reduced to flour, to eat afterward during the winter. Some Spaniards jokingly call this the second pitaja harvest.

Those barbarians who live in the northern part of the peninsula have found the secret, unknown to most mortals, of eating and eating repeatedly the same tidbit. They tie a mouthful of meat which is dried and hardened in the sun securely with a string; they put it in their mouths, and after having chewed it a little, they swallow it, allowing the string to hang from the mouth; they keep it in their stomachs two or three minutes and then pull it up.

–Don Francisco Javier Clavigero (1753)
(Found in *The History of* [Lower] *California* by Clavigero.
Translated by Sara Lake. Edited by A. S. Gray)

There are many reasons why the cruise of the Comfort was most enjoyable, and among them is the fact the Comfort was the first sailing yacht to accomplish such an undertaking. Every day brought its novelties and delights. Even the sunrises and sunsets were gorgeous, multicolored surprises. Nowhere else could be seen such wonderful exhibitions of color tints, and nowhere else does cloudland furnish so many changing formations of sky islands, tinted as they were by the golden rays and spires of light of a departing day or rising sun. And the nights, the glorious silvery nights of that fairy land, lighted by the fires of heaven so thickly distributed that another could not be placed without marring the beauty of the panorama, and burning so brightly that the glimmer of the lamps of man seemed to fade in comparison. Nights when the moonlight clothed nature with a sliver glow. Nights that were light enough to read a newspaper. Nights that were more beautiful than could be described. Nights that are never to be forgotten.

–C. G. Conn (1908)

Of a hundred glorious sunsets there can be no justice in choosing one to remember and describe—yet there was the night, when in the soft bosom of Viscaino rose slowly to draw herself the passionate embrace of a descending globe of fire and framed a nuptial bed with the glories of paradise. Color and temperament. No less in magnificence was the peace of the pearly blue above the cloud line than was the malignity of the snarling, hissing [Sacramento] reef. No whiter were the fluffs of nimbus that hovered in benediction than were the foamy lines of hate that crashed on the mausoleum. Was the ocean green? Were its waters blue? They changed as crimson turned to orange and carmine into pink. Shafts of living flame swept across the sky or rushed to deck the sun and open into a diadem such as no queen has ever worn.

And then the fading, for such a wonder cannot endure. Slowly was the toga drawn aside and the banked clouds adorned themselves with the cast off shreds of a rainbow. Of what avail to note a color? A fleeting instant and it was gone, to be replaced with a tint that surpassed perfection. Even the reef quieted under the spell of celestial pyrotechnics as the disc of pulsating blood, emerging from its last veil, stood revealed, naked and glorious. Then did the courtiers swerve from laughter to tears, then did the lesser lights succumb, and then the stronger, until ghoulish evanescent twilight seized her flash of triumph.

The "Least Petrel" alone was unappreciative. She plugged on, a point east of south, maintaining an even pace for her thirteen hour run ...

–Griffing Bancroft (1930)

THE SONG OF SONORA

(first 8 stanzas)

In far away Southland's grey desert of sand
Beneath wavered plumb-lines of glittering fire
With shadowless sahuaros on Adair Bay stand
Mesquite, ocotillo and cholla and brier.

Sharp tined is each limb, every branch is a foe
Fierce snarling with hate lest some suffering soul
Athirst and aflame in the furnaced-white flow
Should ask the bare pittance of life-giving toll.

'Tis into these wastes I, intruding appear
I crunch through the silt-crust with arrogant stride
While brew their black magic to waken my fear
The imps of the Desert repelled my pride.

They summon wan vampires to poignarded mews
They tauten thronged branches that I may not pass
Divesting my footsteps they seek to confuse
And bring my ruin the power of mass.

Horizons alone mark the ends of the line
Of guardsmen they arm with dread halbert and spike
Cardones overhead threat with limbs grim of spine
They prey on the maze of all pathways alike.

Afoot, traitor half-domes inviting caress
Are aiding Hell's minions to force me to flee
The cholla cast loose its Gorgonian tress
The wilderness closes to bring me to knee.

Vain sprites of the sandhills, I came not to plead
To slaves I shall bend to the strength of my will
Brows wet with the toil that is gauged by my need
I'll lash ye to frenzy that ye may fulfill

Oh Fool that I was to have thought that the Gods
Intended to yield more than one hour's play
They heedlessly cast me impossible odds
When Heaven was opened and closed in a day.

–Griffing Bancroft (1929)

The beauty became most apparent shortly after sun-up. On the rolling hills around us were many lordly cardon, giant agave plants, ocotillo, cirio trees, and thousands upon thousands of wild flowers. In the clear dry atmosphere, the great Sierras seem surprisingly close and behind us the vast silent melancholy of the Chapala plain.

Now quite confident we would soon come to Agua Leon, we stopped for a drink of water and a breakfast of corned beef and tortillas and at the same time, to enjoy, for a change, the delights of nature at its best.

The weather, in its perfection, was genial and enlivening. In an atmosphere of perfect transparency, a few light feathery clouds were visible in a deep blue sky, and spread out around us was the greenery that comes to semi-arid deserts at certain elevations in the early spring. Mourning doves, which so often can be heard but not easily seen, were cooing to each other from all directions.

Otherwise silent and without human habitation, it was to us, a region of adventure over which few white men had trod on foot as we had.

–Howard Hale (1921)

Palmer

There is no more sharply defined faunal and floral area, that occurs to me now, excepting that of islands, than is embraced in the region above defined [Cape Region of Baja California]. Part of it lies within the Tropic of Cancer, and the balance along the Gulf shore and having mainly a Gulf drainage. The climate as influenced by its peculiar sea-bound tropical situation and rainy seasons is distinctively different from anything existing to the northward, but the climatic peculiarities will be noticed beyond. Mainly a mountainous section, some of the peaks being 6,000 feet high, it is separated for an hundred miles or more from the peninsula northward by a long expanse of low, level, or rolling country. Such isolation combined with other causes makes it a region of peculiar scientific interest to both zoologists and botanists.

–Walter E. Bryant (1891)

On September 29 of this rapidly passing year of 1683 we set sail from the port of San Lucas in Sinaloa, bound for the largest island in the world.

–Eusebio Francisco Kino (1683)

In 1536 when Cortés was searching feverishly for a strait which he believed would be found to connect the Pacific with the Atlantic, he sailed northward from Tehuantepec and discovered Baja California. Some of the men in his expedition carried back to Mexico City marvelous tales of an island inhabited by sirens guarded by fierce and gigantic Amazons. This was too much for Francisco de Ulloa; he set forth at once to find the luring maidens, and in his search for the mythical island he discovered Magdalena Bay,

This beautiful arm of the Pacific, forty miles long by twelve miles broad, is shut in by the rocky and irregular Santa Margarita Island. It was long the rendezvous of pirates and was their place of frequent refuge. Drake sought shelter there from a furious hurricane which swept the Pacific; in a secluded cove; Woods brought in a captured Spanish galleon. It is claimed that in undreamed-of caves on Santa Margarita Island much of the pirate gold was hidden and never reclaimed.

Whether because of these tales of buccaneer days, whether because of the mineral wealth of the peninsula, or whether because of the fascination of its immense unknown areas, there is a strange lure about Baja California. Certainly there is beauty in the lagoon-fringed shore of the gulf and the rocky coast of the ocean; there is beauty even in the desolation of the bare brown mountains.

–Vernon Quinn (1938)

The dunes, the moonlight, the festivity, and the champagne all conspired to lead me to the water's edge. Where, weaving pleasantly, I observed our skiff leaving, unattended, on the night tide.

On arriving at the skiff's bow line, I was immediately distracted by the fascinating patterns of bioluminescence that trailed off the rope, my hands, my body. Floating in the warm water, glowing like a firefly, I could hear around me the explosive exaltations and the sonorous inhalations of hundreds of whales as they dreamt leviathan dreams. Some produced an organ-like tone that would have made the Phantom of the Opera proud. Others were more breathy, some had a "hitch," and one seemed to produce two notes at once, a talent formerly found only within the realm of Tibetan monks. Upon realizing I could no longer see the glow of the matrimonial campfire, but was beginning to pick up the sound of crashing surf, I scrambled aboard and started the outboard.

When the moon is full in Magdalena Bay, there is no horizon. The edge of the water blends seamlessly with the dunes and mangroves that define the shore ... I could identify constellations from their reflections, so still was the bay's mirror surface. It was a singular moment; the moonlight, the warm air, the sensation of floating across a bottomless sky. With hardly a ripple, a tall, black wall arose from the watery stars in front of me. With no time to react, I watched dumbfounded, snapping my head around as I passed. At its base, a single huge eye, reflecting the moonlight, watched me skim past.

–Kent Madin (1994)

As we head out to sea, I sight back to the horizon line on shore, always uneven, as a child tears coarse construction paper to make mountains—some steep, some gradual, but always rough, always ragged, always softened by the light into haunting mysterious presences. Is this what the sailors who first saw this coastline saw—a gentle rim of mountains floating over light-filled valleys, a promising beauty that dissolved into brutal reality which for some of them, became final reality? How many stood, straddle-legged on the deck, steadied against the swell, glass to eye and tried to see the promised glint of gold? Or wondered at such a bleak and empty place?

–Ann Zwinger (1983)

The first grey light was enough to awaken me and I was out on the edge of the meadow with my sketchbook. The blue-grey sage with its purple flowers was damp with the night's dew. The miracle began. The soft glow over the granite ridge to the east became stronger and suddenly a shaft of gold broke across the meadow and the picacho glowed a warm rose as if from an inner light. I knew as I watched and sketched, that the painting would be a good one.

–John Hilton (1952)

Palmer

The Sea of Cortez on Baja's east coast is a body of water about 700 miles long, 100 to 150 miles wide and over 4000 feet deep.

There are places, in the southern half of the Sea of Cortez especially, where the underwater topography is amazingly steep. It is almost as if the Baja peninsula is a giant fishing pier sticking out into the Pacific Ocean. In these places, pods of marlin, sailfish, tuna, dorado, and wahoo come to within one to five miles of shore, even closer.

In the reefs, 10 to 300 feet deep, are huge seabass types such as jewfish, grouper, snapper, pargo and cabrilla. Top middleweights found within 500 yards of shore include roosterfish, amberjack, jack crevalle, yellowtail, sierra, corvina, pompano and triggerfish. In places are hordes of barracuda, bass and skipjack. Colorful reef fishes are everywhere among the rocks in blue-green waters.

–Neil Kelly and Gene Kira (1988)

The color of the water changed, in the ocean it was blue, and now in the Gulf of California it is green-gray. I noted on the round world voyage, in the voyage to northern California, and now in southern California, that there where the color of the water has the above coloring, which is mainly in gulfs, straits, bays, the water lights up strongly at night.

–I. G. Voznesenskii (1842)

It has a near resemblance to the Adriatic, a branch of the Mediterranean formed by the coast of Italy, and that of Dalmatia in Greece. The ancient discoverers called it Mar Bermejo, and Mar Roxo, the Red Sea, from its resembling in form, and sometimes in colour and appearance, the Gulf of Arabia, which runs from Suez, betwixt the Coasts of Africa and Asia. It has also been called Mar de Cortez, in compliance with the solicitude of the conqueror of the Mexican empire, in order to augment the glory of his enterprises.

–Padre Miguel Venegas (1757)

Palmer

The entrance is about a League to the Eastward of a round, sandy, bald Headland, which some take to be Cape St. Lucas, because it is the Southernmost Land; but I believe that to be Cape St. Lucas which bears E. by S. from this bald Head, distant about three leagues, and in the Easternmost Point. When you are in the offing, the land makes like an Island off the said Cape.

When you come from the Westward, and are bound in here, the Marks are four high Rocks, the two Westernmost sharp and tapering like a Sugar-loaf; the innermost of the two has an Arch, like that of a Bridge, thro' which the Sea has a Passage, leaving the outermost Rock about half a Cable's Length without you.

–Edward Cooke (1712)

Palmer

As a beach on which to swim—or land a boat—the cove has no peer. The sand lies at so steep an angle that two or three steps give swimming depth. A clear bottom is this, with water fresh from an untainted ocean. Comfortably warm all winter long and refreshing in hot summer days, here should be the site of a great resort. The world does not have so much to offer that man can spare this little gem to emptiness and reverie.

–Griffing Bancroft (1930)

THE PUMA DRINKS THE NEW MOON

(stanzas 30-40)

The gray whales are breaching
Bahia Magdalena has given birth.

Airborne
Manta rays leap toward the sun
The sea is happy.

The Dorado distills sunshine and foam
It's golden aquamarine.

The blue marlin navigates alone
He is a deep sea voyager.

An osprey
On the north wind
Its fish—a weather vane—
Sharp talon.

Racing crabs outpace our footprints
And the surf washes over the sand.

Blue parrotfish nibble the corral
The current bends the purple fans.

A Rock Beauty flirts
With a spider crab
A moray swims scenting blood.

Rooster fish
Streaming silver dorsals
Herd Spanish grunt
Absolutely.

Flying pelicans
Rising and falling
The sun is also setting.

–Ben Stoltzfus (2000)

Mexicans call it el Mar de Cortez, and U.S. maps label it the Gulf of California. But on the old maps sketched with quill pens by early Spanish explorers, it is called el Mar Bermejo, the Vermilion Sea. Some have claimed that this name derives from the famous "red tides" which sometimes fill the gulf with a myriad of tiny creatures that can turn the ocean blood-red. But when I awoke to my first dawn over the Bay of Angels, the rising sun was spreading vermilion across the sky and sea, and the mountains burned with gold vermilion flames. I knew then the Vermilion Sea had been named by someone awakening on just such a morning long ago to just such a sunrise over Bahía De Los Angeles.

–Judy Goldstein Botello (1998)

Spearfishing was the central reason for coming to Baja but it shortly became for me a secondary attraction to the incomparable setting of the Gulf. Never had I imagined such a place. There were as many birds in the sky as fish in the sea, terns by the thousands, gulls of several varieties flying in packed flocks, pelicans gliding in tight formations and stretching in lines for fifty miles or more, albatross and frigates floating on steady wings high in the invisible thermo clines.

Even the osprey appears, circling her fortress of a nest built on the exposed outcrop of a high cliff. The air and sea pulsate with more life than I thought could exist in one place. Standing in mute contrast are the primordial volcanic mountains that lie stripped of vegetation in colors of red rust and chalky granite, the colors vibrating against the blinding blue of the Baja sky.

–Carlos Eyles (1991)

Flying fish scud across unrippled waters soaring as high as twenty feet on occasion. But more often leaving a tiny, thin wake as they flutter just above the surface, using only their tails as rudders. The fighting albacore make its home as far north as Bahia de Los Angeles sharing the area with the barracuda. Giant devilfish leap unexpectedly in a surge of swirling foam, crashing back again with a splat! audible for miles. This is the northernmost point that the roosterfish venture, but throughout the Gulf there are porpoises and nearly every remote, rocky headland harbors a noisy sea lion rookery.

The Gulf abounds with shark, from the big man-eating hammerheads down to the smaller but no less ferocious sand shark. Huge schools of black sea bass, tuna, halibut, mullet, and red snappers cruise in their common search for food. Down in the deeps lurk the groupers, feeding off anything that drifts down their way. Sailfish, yellowtail, yellowfin tuna, and of course, striped and black marlin are the favorite choice of fishermen.

In no less abundance are white sea bass, surfperch, sablefish, lingcod, corbina, bonefish, croaker, and cabrilla ... Out in the deep water swim the California grey whales, relentlessly pursued by killer sharks.

–Spencer Murray (1960)

Many a cruiser has likened the Sea of Cortez, or the Gulf of California as it is also called, to a moonscape. There is little doubt of the origin of the islands, as they are frozen in time: you can almost picture the rugged cliffs being suddenly cooled to form their honeycombed appearance or envision the huge boulders being flung about by volcanic blasts.

Cactus and elephant trees dot the rock formations which rise dramatically from the turquoise sea. The overall effect is surreal, taking you backwards through time, to when the earth split and the rift flooded with water to form this beautiful gulf.

–Elizabeth Maul Schwartz (2003)

The savage inhabitants of California were slightly different in their manner of living from the animals described. But if we study those few vestiges of antiquity which remain there, we shall be persuaded, perhaps, that this vast peninsula was inhabited previously by less barbaric peoples than the ones whom the Spaniards found in it because the Jesuits, in the last years that they were there, discovered in the mountains situated between latitude 27 and 28, various large caves made in enduring rock and figures of decently dressed men and women and different kinds of animals painted on the walls ...

Now these pictures and clothing are not characteristic of those brutish and savage nations which inhabited California when the Spaniards reached it. They belong without doubt, to another ancient nation, but we are unable to say what it was. The Californians affirm unanimously that these pictures were the work of a giant-like nation which had come there from the North

–Don Francisco Javier Clavigero (1786)

California began as a geographic myth, an insular place on the right hand of the Indies. Then it became the line of misty peaks which scarred the sunsets as the Conquistadors looked west. In the mid-Eighteenth Century, California still meant only the peninsula and many thought of it as an island. Two or three Jesuit missionaries, toiling in this most rocky of vineyards, made surprising finds of ancient art. During two centuries their little-known accomplishment was augmented at long intervals by the efforts of a French chemist and an American writer of detective fiction. This oddly-assorted group carries the flag, beats the drum and sounds the fife for a slowly gathering parade back to the places and times of the painters.

In the Sierras of central Baja California, hidden by a most forbidding terrain, thousands of brilliant paintings survive in caves and shelters. Here a prehistoric people created giant images, assemblages of heroic men and animals. Their time passed, they laid down their brushes and disappeared, their art was lost to sight and their existence was reduced to the breath of a legend.

–Harry Crosby (1975)

From the summer of 1540 when Hernando de Alarcon, one of Cortez's admirals, finding the surrounding sea swarming with voracious sharks, gave the land its name, Tiburon Island has been a place of ill repute amongst men. A race of splendid physique and marvelous fleetness, its inhabitants, known as the Seri, were reported by Don Rodrigo Maldonado, an officer of Coronado, as being "so large and tall that the best man in the [Spanish] army reached only to their chests." It is no wild phantasy to surmise that Tiburon is really the island which Cortez had in view when he sent his admirals in search of California, "the land of the Amazons;" certainly the Seri women exercise an unusual control of affairs on Tiburon, and all kinship is reckoned in the female line.

Prior to the middle of the seventeenth century the inhabitants of the island were reputed to be cannibals, a stigma which still attaches to them; by the opening of the eighteenth century their animosity toward strangers had become proverbial. Neighboring Indian tribes, Spaniards, Mexicans, Americans, indeed, all visiting aliens have found the Seri inexplicably treacherous and hostile. Non-agricultural barbarians, scantily garbed in pelican skins, partial to meat uncooked and to the unspeakably disgusting "second crop" of the cacti, these isolated aborigines are possessed of a pride of blood so fierce and intense that to intermingle their own with that of an alien is an indefensible crime.

–Arthur W. North (1910)

Palmer

These cowboys wore leather protective pants, boots, and wide brimmed stiff leather hats. Their saddles and bridles were things of beauty and all made in this part of the country by local craftsmen ...

The cowboys assured us that very soon now, the cattle, all young bulls, would be coming and that they were all in a hurry to take the bath while swimming out to the boat ...

Two men got into the boat, one in the bow and one in the stern. The boat, with the two bulls attached, was manhandled into the water until it floated ...

At first the bulls simply walked beside the boat to which they were tethered, but as the water deepened, they began to swim; their heads tied securely above the water. They had to swim as they were pulled along ...

When the first boat reached the side of the ship, a cable attached to the boom of a power winch was hooked to a rope around the horns of the bull and he was lifted high in the air and lowered into the hold of the vessel. When the second bovine was in the air, the two men started rowing back to shore for another pair of "swimming bulls."

–Pel Carter (1967)

But if Father Palou did have his miracles I once had my vision. Or rather a lot of them. And they turned out real. This again was down in Baja California where so much of the present is still our past, or our past is still their present, however we care to word it. Yet when down there in the harsh interior I saw Mexican cowboys wearing the same kind of leather trappings which had been worn by our own California vaqueros of a century or more ago.

Nobody had tipped me off that this would be the case. This added to the surprise. For the riders down there were not on parade, or anything like that. This was no deliberate show. The riders, riding alone, most of them, were merely out in their own thorny country rounding up stray stock or herding stock from one waterhole to another in that fenceless interior.

Most of these riders were days and days apart, miles and miles apart. Though the riders did not wear silver spangles, as in our theatrical pageants, the riders certainly were protected with heavy leather from their shoulders to below the stirrups.

–Max Miller (1951)

Palmer

Isla Raza is a nesting ground admirably suited to the breeding habits of terns, gulls, petrel, pelicans, grebes, and other species that return to the island year after year in response to an unvarying primordial instinct; it is the setting for tens of thousands of breeding pairs of seabirds between April and June of each season. During this period the birds literally cover every square inch of available space on the flat surface of the land with their nests and eggs.

At one time every canoe and boat, within miles of Raza Island, capable of navigating across the intervening waters from the Peninsular coast was paddled out to this bird island; egg collectors bent on scooping up a valuable boat load for sale in the coastal markets of San Felipe, Santa Rosalia, Mulege, La Paz, Guaymas and Hermosillo. Each egger in the course of the season was responsible for taking as many as from 30,000 to 50,000 eggs, a quantity, when multiplied by the number of eggers, that the bird population could not accommodate and survive.

–Leland Lewis (1971)

On the eastern edge of Ventana Bay, Deborah and I paddle over to a shipwrecked steamer, shoved onto the ivory sand by the northerlies. The water is transparent jade and as I come to the stern of the shipwreck, five large and lifeless forms appear on the tideline, clouded with jenenes. The air smells of salt, so the carnage is fresh. I jump out; they're mantas. The wings of these five-foot-wide, several hundred pound beings have been skinned alive for meat—perhaps twenty pounds per animal. The scene is remarkably familiar, and when I recall all the fishermen who told me how prolific the mantas used to be several years ago, it evokes the buffalo herds inundating the vast American plains ...

The white-bellied, black-topped manta I couch next to was dumped here only hours ago. The meat from its wing bottom was carved out with a sharp knife—the manta grunting like a bear as chunks of flesh were ripped out and a reddened fan of delicate bones was exposed to the merciless orb of the sun.

–Jonathan Waterman (1994)

The first time I tried my large seine we captured about 3000 pounds in a few pulls, and my heart bursted nearly when I had to trow [sic] them away, so beautiful they were.

–John Xantus (1859)

… But whatever the divine intentions, or the geologist's theories about the creation of this new gulf—a warm water paradise year 'round—it brings an indescribable jubilation to today's fishermen.

The warm waters of the Pacific rushed in and the peninsula made a perfect "gate" for the trap. Every kind of fish—plus mammals—that found their way from the Pacific into this new gulf came exploring its many wonders. The current that carried Hoei-Sin probably helped too. Most of 'em liked the balmy temperatures of the surface waters—or they could choose the cool, cool depths at the bottom where the San Andreas split went two miles deep.

More than 850 species have now been classified in the Gulf of California. There may be even more. Level on level they find their favorite depths (and for cafeteria they have only to swim up to the floor above.) Biggest of course, are the whales who swim in around the Cape from the Pacific and half way up the gulf for their own smorgasbord.

It has been pointed out by geologists and ichthyologists that the whole cycle of the Gulf's fish life is aided and abetted by the fact that the Colorado River has, for thousands of years, been emptying its silt and nutrient riches from the watershed of the American Rocky Mountains. Here are the phosphates, nitrates, organic materials to feed the bacteria that feed the plankton that feed the insects and lower forms of marine life that feed, in turn, the graduating larger sizes of fish. All these riches are unending resources for centuries to come.

It's a fish trap unequaled in all the World.

–Mike McMahan (1973)

The most exciting of all experiences that I have ever been involved in, on land or sea was a fish pileup in the Sea [of Cortez]. These extravagant mass murders occur during spring migrations. They are triggered when long schools of hungry yellowtail mixed with armies of bonito and skipjack, collide with an ever greater concentration of sardines, herring, and other small fishes abounding in the cooler Midriff waters. As the game fish cross the convergent line of warm and cold waters, the smaller fishes take to the air in such numbers they form what seems to be a solid blanket two to three feet above the surface.

It is then that every fish-eating creature of the Sea dashes into the fray and runs amok, chomping or disemboweling each other in a ferocious frenzy. As a result of this devastating interruption in the well-ordered processes of evolution, the normally calm, lipid face of the Sea is churned in convulsion of mass slaughter. There appears to be a sudden reversal in time, halting all the rhythmic balances developed by nature over millions of years.

–Ray Cannon (1966)

Palmer

With the nets which every ship carried, a great quantity of fish of many species and different forms, all very good, wholesome, and of good taste, was caught each day. That it may be known what the kinds of fish were, I give here the names of those I saw and had in my hands; sardines, chermas, red-snapper, perch, cornudos, dog fish, skate, salmon, tunny, esmeregales, oysters, ray-fish, chuchos, mackerel, roncodors, mutton-fish, bonitos, puercos, sole, sirgueros, newt, a great quantity of pearl oysters, and many whales ...

The devil-fish are so large that one of them wrapped itself around the cable of the anchor-buoy with which the Almiranta was made fast, pulled it up and made off with it and the ship, so that it was necessary to kill it, but a large number of soldiers and sailors who were pulling it with strong ropes never succeeded in getting it out on land from the water. The mouth is like a half-moon, seven spans across from one side to the other, and from the head to the tail it measures seventeen spans.

–Antonio de la Ascension (16[illegible]2)

When a rooster fish takes the bait, let it run. Give it time to stop and turn the bait in its mouth; set the hook and hang on!

It will strip off the line at an alarming rate. And if it's on the surface, it will set up a roostertail like the wake of a high-powered speedboat. On the light tackle it may jump at the end of the run, snapping its head like a tarpon. After you get it turned and regain some line, be prepared for another vicious run, and another, and another. It will then sound and fight with the endurance of a shark. About the time you see the rooster, it will see the boat, get the general idea of what you have in mind, and make another run almost as long as its original effort. Of one thing you can be certain: if you get a rooster fish to gaff, he is whipped, they never give up!

–Jerry Klink (1974)

Palmer

We cling to the anchor line, human dive flags flapping in the Sea of Cortez's underwater breeze. Safety stop. Dive over. A shadow as wide as a cruise ship drifts by. I look up and my mask plate is filled with white spots and blue skin. A whale shark is swimming through us like we're laundry on his line.

Behind a goatee of remoras I can see his long grin. Is it a mockery? A friendly greeting? The sweet contentment of knowing you're the biggest fish in what has been called the world's richest sea? He lumbers past us like a mile-long freight train, disappearing into the vague blue distance. Mental Note: In the Sea of Cortez, Señor Big favors you with a visit when you least expect it.

They say you're not supposed to come down here looking for the big stuff—manta rays with 20-foot wingspans and clearance to land at O'Hare, whale sharks, schooling hammerheads, marlins taller than Manute Bol. They say over fishing has made encounters with Señor Big too unpredictable. Content yourself with 250 species of reef fish and 750 species of other fish—more fish of different sizes, shapes and colors than just about anywhere else on the planet.

–Jim Sommers (1994)

We had only a 12-foot boat mounted on top of our jeep, with a 10-horse outboard to power it. At Cabo San Lucas, we launched it and set out to see the sea where the blue Pacific waters lapped into the edge of the Gulf.

Trolling along with a 60-pound line and a dead mackerel for bait, we hooked up with this handsome, big swordfish beauty. He went zing. He plunged. We reeled in just a little. Up he came and—pow! Straight into the air to see if we were still around.

Then off he went again, pulling our 12-foot boat like a toy. We held on for dear, sweet life. Down again. Up! Then he turned racing for shore. Fine! Just the way we wanted to go ...

Whooaaaa! He slowed down. Reel him in, Tom! Hold it! He's off again! The blue Pacific now was calling him. Him, not us.

And this time he didn't stop. The boat bounced over the waves. Our decision came fast: we cut the line ...

–Mike McMahan (1933)

The chief place of resort, however, was at the headwaters of the lagoon [Scammon's] ... Here the objects of pursuit were found in large numbers, and here the scene of slaughter was exceedingly picturesque and unusually exciting, especially on a calm morning, when the mirage would transform not only the boats and their crews into fantastic imagery, but the whales, as they sent forth their towering spouts of aqueous vapor, frequently tinted with blood, would appear quite distorted ...

In February, 1856, we found two whales aground in Magdelena Bay. Each had a calf playing about, there being sufficient depth for the young ones, while the mothers were lying hard on the bottom. When attacked, the smaller of the two old whales lay motionless, and as the boat approached near enough to 'set' the hand-lance into her 'life,' dispatching the animal at a single dart. The other, when approached would raise her head and flukes above the water, supporting herself on a small portion of the belly, turning easily, and heading toward the boat ...

It appears to be their habit to get into the shallowest inland waters when their cubs are young.

–Captain Charles Scammon (1856)
(Found in *The Forgotten Peninsula* by Joseph Wood Krutch.)

"CLANG-CLANG," rang the ship's bell. "Melly Kissmass. Blekfast soon leddy. Mebbe catch a big fish today," shouted the Japanese steward as he thrust his head above the hatchway. With these pleasantries and with everybody feeling cheerful and Happy, Christmas day of 1908 was ushered into existence aboard the sailing yacht Comfort as she lay at anchor in San Bartolome Bay.

At the entrance of the bay, just off the big kelp bed will be found the home of the giant sea bass, or Jew fish as they are commonly called. The fishing ground had already been exploited by the anglers of the Comfort and it was decided that Christmas day should be devoted to taking a catch of black sea bass for photographic purposes ...

The big fish were in waiting and the sport began as soon as the first bait touched water. Fun, did you say? Well, if straining every muscle of one's body in a strenuous effort to wear out a finny monster, weighing from one to three hundred pounds by pumping and reeling him up to the boat after and hour's endeavor, then it is fun to catch a big black sea bass with a rod and reel. [Ed. note: 16 of the giant sea bass were taken solely for "photographic purposes."]

–C. G. Conn (1908)

The sweet smell of the land blew out to us on a warm wind, a smell of sand verbena and grass and mangrove. It is so quickly forgotten, this land smell. We know it so well on shore that the nose forgets it, but after a few days at sea the odor memory pattern is lost so the first land smell strikes a powerful emotional nostalgia, very sharp and strangely dear.

In the morning the black mystery of the night was gone and the little harbor was shining and warm.

–John Steinbeck (1940)

Palmer

Sometimes in the night a little breeze springs up and the boat tugs experimentally at the anchor and swings slowly around. There is nothing so quiet as a boat when the motor has stopped; it seems to lie with held breath. One gets to longing for the deep beat of the cylinders.

–John Steinbeck (1940)

Palmer

Then, over a sand dune, we saw it for the first time [Malarrimo Beach.] Against the setting sun—that come hither star of every explorer—the evening's fog wisped and rolled and flirted with the beach. And look at that beach! The prow of an ancient boat—maybe three or four hundred years old ...

All about: the blue-green glass balls, escaped from float duty on Nippon fishing nets to travel half way 'round the world. And driftwood from a dozen distant forests. Amidst all this: tins and tins of army rations. Candy we found, cigarettes in waterproof containers and foods of all kinds.

And look! A torpedo! Alive or dead we did not know ...

Over there, steamer deck chairs and the wreckage of a plane. Sure enough, Malarrimo was not a very safe landing strip. And there were hatch covers by the dozens ... But that night the hatch covers made the best sort of wind-break for our camp fire on the beach. We decided to try out the corned beef in one of the tins along with the coffee from another. Good! There were plenty of lifeboat emergency drinking water tins for the coffee, too.

–Mike McMahan (1983)

We've paced off a 30 foot redwood log, certainly not indigenous to this area, and stomped around on the wooden deck of a ship. One of our group discovered a partially buried airplane, another a Cadillac Coupe de Ville. Ed found a bottle tossed off a ship as a scientific experiment of "National Geographic World" and Trent uncovered another bottle from a California girl looking for a pen pal. So Malarrimo was all we'd imagined. We still have an unopened gas mask canister and the bright orange hatch cover from a ship; today it frames a photo of our group of Malarrimo explorers.

–Patti and Tom Higginbotham (1996)

I could have done with a supermarket trolley as I wandered along the beach [Malarrimo] picking up several cans of beer, coke, lifeboat rations, shampoo, sunscreen, contraceptives, spray cans of pasteurized cheese, and cream, not to mention biscuits from Spain, dried snacks from Japan, chocolate syrup from Hershey's ...

I was struggling on, weighed down with bottles of Bacardi, Scotch, brandy and Japanese whisky when I spied a nearly full bottle of London Gin ... After toasting Queen and Empire I continued on my wobbly path.

–Graham Mackintosh (1985)

The information which I had received at San Francisco led me to believe that the country was a verdant plain, abounding in fine pastures and running streams. I was grievously disappointed. My guides had no knowledge of any fresh water except on the trail to Commundo, which makes a detour through the interior, at a considerable distance from the coast. This trail passes over a desert region, prolific only in cactus and thorny shrubs. Blind trails, made by wild animals, branch off from it in every direction; and it is exceedingly difficult even for an experienced guide to avoid losing the way. The whole face of the earth for a hundred miles or more, north and south, and eastward across the peninsula, is a complication of rugged mountains of a sedimentary formation, and mesas cut into fearful arroyos and ravines by the floods of former times, and stretches of sand desert.

All the vegetation visible to the eye seems to conspire against the intrusion of man. Every shrub is armed with thorns; the cactus, in all its varieties, solitary and erect, or in twisted masses, or snake-like undulations, tortures the traveler with piercing needles and remorseless fangs. Burs with barbed thorns cover the ground; the very grass, wherever it grows resents the touch with wasp-like stings that fester in the flesh; and poisonous weeds tempt the hungry animals with their verdure producing craziness and death.

Add to this the innumerable varieties of virulent reptiles and insects that infest those desolate regions in summer; the sand-flies, the rabid polecats that creep around the camp-fire at night, producing hydrophobia by their bite; the scorching heat of the sun, and the utter absence of water, and you have a combination of horrors that might well justify the belief of the old Spaniards that the country was accursed by God.

–John Ross Browne (1867)

Palmer

April 27, 1849. All day, the so-called road was over a table mountain. The most barren region imaginable. The earth or rather the rocks have been convulsed in a singular manner and piled fantastically one on another. They could not be more rugged. Over such a country we picked a difficult way, depressed by the suffering of our poor horses, and the utter desolation around us.

Unexpectedly we came to the margin of a great chasm. Some one said, "See this is Comondu." Looking down there lay, some 200 feet below us, a perfect picture. A beautiful little valley green as an emerald, while the sunlight glancing from water fairly made the very horses laugh. Impulsively we scrambled down the barranca side at a breakneck pace and soon arrived to the satisfaction of man and beast. We were tired out but here we now are enjoying plenty of food and sweet water, and our poor horses are reveling up to their knees in green grass.

–W. C. S. Smith (1849)

There is no sun like the sun that shines
    In the Valley of Comondú.

    There are palms and olives and figs and vines
    In the Valley of Comondú.

–Author and date unknown

I'll let the rest of the world take Santa Rosalía, San Ignacio, Mulegé, and certainly La Paz, if only the rest of the world will concede me Comondú. Little, hidden Comondú, the mountain-snuggled hamlet which, if given my choice, I would wish to visit first on going back.

Comondú, hidden these several centuries with the Sierra de la Giganta, is a delicate little sermon on the art of minding one's own business. The villagers are self-sustaining. They have their own dates, their own sugarcane, their own figs, their own grapes, and the best mountain water in all the land. We may call such people rustics if we like, but they do have the answer to something.

Comondú is one of those unspoiled little Mexican villages which can make an American feel gross and awkward, no matter what he does. The villagers do not especially want the pesos that the visitor has to spend and the children are untrained in the art of begging.

–Max Miller (1941)

A warm spring, giving abundance of water with a strong sulphurous odor, which after cooling loses its smell and becomes drinkable, once irrigated were the agricultural lands there (now abandoned). The aspect of the mountains surrounding the mission [San Borja] is altogether mineral. They cultivated in former times corn, wheat, beans, and there are yet to be seen in the deserted gardens fig, olive and pomegranate trees, and dates, mescal, and palm trees innumerable.

The streams of Los Angeles abound in fish. There are not cattle, but nature has compensated for their absence by innumerable herds of deer and mountain goats. The Church is of the order of San Javier, but is now almost in ruins. The best oil paintings and a few silver ornaments, were taken therefrom in accordance with superior instructions. The church experienced the same fate as that of Santa Gertrudis, during the emigration to Upper California.

Eight Indians, one 108 years old, and another 104 years of age, are the only inhabitants of that otherwise deserted place.

–Sebastian Viosca (1863)

DESERT ROAD

Walking in a bowl of dust
rimmed with cool ceramic blue
above the lip of mountains.
Fine dirt talcum powders my toes,
fills my mouth, dries my breath,
and coats my skin lightly,
so that the cardon and I
wear a thin jacket of earth.

–Jennifer Redmond (1999)

All along the Gulf slopes of the Sierra de San Francisco one encounters a profusion of twisted torote and swollen cardón. Visitors have found them grotesque from the first, and they remain strange even with long acquaintance. Gradually, however, a thoughtful traveler comes to appreciate the vertical relief they provide to the landscape, their prosperity in a land of so little promise, and their rugged beauty. When the last are finally left behind, there is a void. They are missed.

–Harry Crosby (1974)

Our early introduction to the cactus was merely a formality. We didn't become well acquainted until later. I haven't seen all the curious sights this globe has to offer, so I hope I may not be regarded as too cocksure when I voice the notion that there isn't anywhere, such a spectacle.

How many species of this desert vegetation we saw I wouldn't hazard a guess. Their number passes M. Voltaire's bounds of probability. From the giant cirio and suwarro stretching straight into the heavens for as much as fifty feet they ranged down to the tiny pincushion cactus, not much larger than an egg. Both cirio and suwarro were in bloom. The former tossing their white plumes grandly in the breeze; the latter bearing their crowns of flowers with a more profound stateliness.

–Phil Hanna (1928)

A CALIFORNIO

Down Baja,
alone on a motorcycle,
gasoline my religion.

This morning a jarred faith,
canteens of gas expended,
a sputtering engine.

In the distance, a *vaquero* on his mount
Hollywood hyperbolists, these two,
yet a universe from fiction.

To the *ranchita*
Holy Serum siphoned from a tractor
no words or *dinero* exchanged.

Porch steps on our haunches,
"*Cigarillo*?" my gesture.
"*Uno mas*?" "*uno mas*?"

Again, no words exchanged—
Only smoke and fumes.

–Gregory MacDonald (1969)

ARISTOCRATS OF STONE

El Mármol was a town of pure onyx—including the school house and jail.
Only raised tombs remain—ghostly signals of finality.
Quarried slabs that were solid—forgotten toil, surrendering tonnage.
Trucked on terrain that was hostile—overtaxed axles and springs.

Floated on rafts that were tilting—improbable launching.
Craned onto ships that resisted—unruly monoliths.
Sailed against contrary currents—decks awash.
Unloaded for milling and carving—end of the line.
ARISTOCRATS OF STONE—now ashtrays and bookends

–Gregory MacDonald (1969)

As the first shot rang out two more sheep suddenly appeared and rushed away in the wake of the leader. If you are fond of Nature, dear reader, imagine yourself on a projecting crag with a mighty abyss below and range and range of wild barren sierra beyond; a golden sun tinting the world and warming your blood and Dame Nature in her grandest, most majestic mood pausing beside you. If your life is dear to you imagine yourself filled with vigor, drawing in deep breaths of mountain air, your muscles swelling out like great steel bands and that life which ten minutes earlier seemed about to be forfeited, thrilling you with wild abandon. If you enjoy shooting imagine yourself on the edge of a mesa with nigh a league of fair view before you and three mountain sheep, the noblest creatures of the wilderness, bounding away from you, their great horns held proudly aloft, while your sharp-voiced rifle calls them to a halt.

–Arthur W. North (1906)

I had not expected to find them [bighorn sheep] so quickly ... At the base of the pinnacle, one to the right and two to the left, I could see the heads of the other rams, all looking directly at me. Just as I dropped to my knee to shoot, the setting sun broke through the clouds behind me, gloriously bringing out all the details. The leader was standing almost broadside to me, his massive head accentuated by the deer-like leanness of his neck and body. The shining sun and falling rain had formed a rainbow directly back of the pinnacle on which the ram stood. What a wonderful picture it would have made for an artist like Rungius! That magnificent ram, standing like a statue on the pedestal of red bronze lava, washed by the falling sun; on one side a head with horns quite as massive as those of the central figure, on the other the heads of two younger rams, and the whole group overarched by a gorgeous rainbow! Estimating the distance at three hundred yards, I held slightly over the shoulder of the big ram, and the big ball struck him fair in the heart. His legs doubled under him like a jackknife and he slid off the pinnacle. Striking the rough lava, he turned over twice and then lay still, while his friends, after staring at me a few seconds, disappeared like shadows. As I turned back and picked my way over the fissures and broken lava, I felt like a vandal who had destroyed a beautiful statue ...

–William T. Hornaday (1909)

Palmer

RANCHO MEZQUITAL

Cerca Cansada;
Me siento mal venido.

Weary fence;
I felt unwelcome.

Pozo seco;
Me da sed.

Dry well;
Made me thirsty.

Aire al rojo vivo;
No puedo respirar.

Torched air;
Could not breathe.

Huesos blanqueados;
Pensamientos de muerte lenta.

Bleached bones;
Thoughts of slow dying.

Trigo petrificado;
Punzadas de hambre.

Petrified wheat;
Pangs of starvation.

Carretilla mohosa;
Falta de Fuerzas.

Rusted barrow;
Emasculation.

Tierra agrietada;
Deseperación.

Cracked earth;
Desperation.

–Gregory MacDonald (1997)

LIEUTENANT ROBERT HARDY'S OBSERVATIONS

On the inhabitants of Loreto:

The inhabitants of Loreto are of a dingy, opaque, olive green, which shows that there is no friendly mixture in the blood of the Spaniard and the Indian; or it may be, that by degrees they are returning to the colour of the aborigines. They appear to be the same squalid, flabby, mixed race, which is observed in almost every part of the Mexican coasts. I did not see a good-looking person among them, always excepting the commandant and ci-devant deputy!

It is said that their morals are extremely loose, that the holy friars have their full share in the general corruption; and although marriage is not always dispensed with, it is generally considered by them as a superfluous ceremony.

On El Camino Real:

The road ascends by the ravine till it reaches a very elevated spot on this very "Giantess," and then descends to a depth below, which is frightfully horrible to the unpracticed traveler, and at an angle extraordinarily acute. Scarcely do you begin to descend, before it becomes necessary to check the bridle of the well-taught mule, and by applying the lash at the same time, to oblige the animal to sit down on his haunches. Although trembling, he places his fore legs well forward at the same time, and down slides the mule and traveler like a ship launched from a dry dock into the sea, until they come to a sort of insecure resting place some yards lower down. After this, there will be walk, and then another sliding place, until the mule rests safely on the plain below.

On the holy friar of the mission at Mulegé:

On the 27th I had the honour of entertaining the padre aboard, who came attended by the amiable female companions whom I had seen in his house on my arrival there. He was as talkative as he had been on our first acquaintance, but indulged much less in his favorite polemics. This I chiefly attributed to a few glasses of Spanish cogniac, which he praised in such a way as gave me to understand that he expected to take, at least, a bottle home with him.

Our style of cookery and our viands, which were merely salt beef, biscuit, and beans, were considered dainties too trifling for his reverence's stomach; and, as he frequently complained of coldness in that department, he had recourse so often to the bottle, that gradually in proportion as his tongue became thicker and thicker after each glass, his loquacity gradually subsided into a sort of splutter, and not being able, in consequence, to articulate whole words, by cutting short the last syllable, he composed a sort of jargon, which no sober person could understand.

–Lieutenant Robert Hardy, Royal Navy (1826)

The quiet water of Bahia Pichilinque makes this a good place to varnish a boat or to swim in the turquoise waters. It is also a good place to study the pelicans and the flying fish which flip out of the water at Sundown.

The surface was so still one night that the reflected stars could be seen in their constellations as clearly in the water as in the sky. Orion's belt and dagger were mirrored there, and the Dipper in the water was turned as if to catch liquid from the Dipper in the sky.

–Annette Scott (1971)

We found the great La Paz cringing on her knees in self-pity and mistrust. And in ill-health. Everything of late had gone wrong with her. Now the one-time pearl capital of the Americas was a crouching figure of sadness indeed. Nobody seemed to care about La Paz any more—now that she had lost her pearls.

Nobody toasted her as in the old days. Nobody ever came to see her any more. Nobody seemed to care whether she lived of died. Poor La Paz.

Poor me too. For a distance of something like eleven hundred road miles of rocks and dust and sand and heat I had been expecting something better—a triumphant finale in La Paz.

A mysterious epidemic to the pearl-oyster beds is what caused it. Everybody in La Paz will agree on that part of the tragedy. The pearl-oysters suddenly all died within a single season not very long before my arrival. The beds all died at once, even those which were a hundred miles apart.

–Max Miller (1943)

There is one real humdinger called "no-see-um" or "jenene" that is a very small knat with teeth like a piranha. Its bite itches worse than a mosquito's and lasts for several days. They live near the high tide line on sandy beaches in warm weather, and they come out in hordes at dusk to eat you up ...

There is another pesky critter found not near camp but out on the water. This is a tiny black fly that lives on bird guano-covered rocks and isles. When the wind dies down and you come too close to their guano, they'll abandon ship and jump all over you, hovering around your eyes and nose by the hundreds. They become very attached to you and will stick with you even if you leave the area. They don't bite, but they crawl all over any exposed skin. You have to remove them physically by scraping them off. They love repellents. Lap it up like syrup.

–Neil Kelly and Gene Kira (1988)

The estuary furnishes a pretty investiture for the pueblo [Mulegé] and a perfect breeding place for the mean malaria mosquito, whose victims we noted parading lethargically about town like so many cadaverous caricatures out of Jugen.

–Phil Hanna (1928)

I sought all around. I went down to the second bar mouth of the river. I saw something like a man's head, and sure enough it was my cook sitting in the water with nothing but his head visible. He had a bunch of grass in one hand and his hat in the other, and blasting the damned country like a pirate. There was no cause but a few million sand flies and mosquitoes. He couldn't stand it and just gave up the ship.

–John F. Janes (1871)

We sleep fitfully under the stars and between our kayaks as scores of inch-long rock roaches (or louses) scurry over us. We could move up higher, but the tickle of roaches, waving antennas in search of algae, is preferable to the snakes or scorpions crawling above.

Scores of ghost crabs scuttle as eight-legged penlights in front of our feet and disappear into holes above the darkened water-line. I step into the tent, but a buzzing like that from a low-frequency beehive prevents me from taking the last step. A rattlesnake is coiled and ready to strike, guarding the door; I jump back; Deborah screams. Under my headlight beam, its eyes glow orange bonfires, its tongue flickers for our scent, its buzzing tail waves ominously.

–Jonathan Waterman (1994)

Down the camino we plunged, followed hard in the wake of our thirst-crazed burros. Some slow dragging moments brought us into the midst of a group of natives lounging in dreamy apathy before the open doorway of a small shack built against the base of a cliff. "Agua, agua!" we demanded, gaspingly, with naught by way of preliminary greeting.

Our hoarse, broken voices, our dry, mumbling lips, our frenzied manner, our burros wading belly-deep in the stream beyond: no need to amplify such signs to children of an arid land, to a people reared amid tragedies of the desert. On the instant, seizing cups and gourds they dipped up cooling water from an earthen olla, splashing our dry faces, our dry necks, our dry arms with large gourds of blessed water, then they gave us each a brimming cup, a great, cooling, life-renewing cup of water, cautioning us the meantime lest we drink overmuch.

And thus I came to San Ignacio, the favored ...

–Arthur W. North (1910)

The road [from San Ignacio] to Santa Rosalia—a rough one—climbs another thousand feet to wind through the lava-built foothills of the six-thousand–foot volcanoes called the Three Virgins—probably the most recently active of the many recent cones in Baja. Then it drops almost a thousand feet to the desert floor in a series of spectacular switch-back curves which Erle Stanley Gardner calls "the road of death" and the natives, hardly less melodramatic, call Cuesta del Infiernillo. In sober fact, the curves are so sharp that on at least one occasion we found it necessary to back up in order to make the turn. The roadway is almost as steep and very little wider than the mule trail down the Grand Canyon.

–Joseph Wood Krutch (1961)

Thousands of towering date palms, many 200 years old, an inviting fresh water lake, and a commanding mission tower rising above both trees and surrounding structures, such is the initial view of the traveler as he emerges from the black hills and sandy plains to note San Ignacio directly below him.

San Ignacio is the most northerly of the lush oasis communities in the southern half of Baja California. It is also the best watered. Large springs pour from barren mountainsides to feed several large ponds, one, a lake of such size that it is crossed on a cause-way. Water from these lakes is diverted into stone-lined ditches to irrigate between 80,000 and 90,000 date palms. Under minimum care since the first plantings back in the 1730's, the palms often grow in forest-like groves.

After the harvest, the dried dates are San Ignacio's principal export crop, but the farms also contain hundreds of orange and fig trees, as well as several vineyards. It is not surprising that the San Ignacians, in their land of perpetual summer, lead comparatively leisurely lives.

–L. Burke Belden (1965)

This was a spot [Coyote Lagoon] not to be neglected. I took my gun and went to get four whitewing dove for our dinner. Accomplishing my mission in short order I took a pail and headed for the mangrove trees. It was low tide and their roots were exposed. Clinging in large clusters to the roots were hundreds of small oysters. I took my machete and hacked off sufficient for an appetizing stew. Returning to camp, the sands by the water's edge seemed to be moving slightly under my feet. Upon investigation I discovered a plentiful supply of fresh clams from three to five inches below the surface. The small butter clams and the larger chocolate clams were in abundance ... Soon there were enough for a tasty oyster stew made with condensed milk. Pat prepared the dove in our pressure cooker, and once done we steamed the clams.

–O. W. Timberman (1959)

Palmer

We were glad to step out into the evening, walk around the plaza, and return to our quarters ... Overhead a balcony resting on an ebon rectangle, a serape across its rail and flower pots under its ceiling. Underfoot a dusty road streaked with ruts and edged with a yard-like footpath, raised. On one side silhouetted trees and a straight line that glistened above the invisible frame of lighted doorways and windows. The other wall was unadorned adobe, a livid sheet of tan that disappeared at either end into a void. Out of the night not a murmur of air, only a gentle laugh or a whispered voice, and then there floated the stringed notes of Rancho Grande.

Across the lunar stage, slipping without gesture out of one shadow and into another, passed a figure, a long-skirted wide-hipped old woman with the carriage of a dragoon under a mantilla that draped from crown to waist. The spotlight shone empty one dramatic moment, then coming unheralded and leaving without pause, walked two white-shirted men, girded with sashes and crowned with high-peaked wide-brimmed sombreros of straw. They pass a child, a girl with the fringe of the black scarf of her sex meeting the hem of her knee-length frock. By one's or two's or three's other figures intermittently parade this bandbox of an arena which is a living pueblo.

It is San Ignacio, the Partner's pride and pet ...

–Griffing Bancroft (1932)

Doubtless it is easy for romanticism to exaggerate and overvalue the simplicities but there is something very real about their attractions. However low the "standard of living" may be, it is also a high one when measured in terms of certain goods not commonly taken into account when the standard of living is discussed.

Though the inhabitants have relatively few time and labor saving machines they seem, paradoxically, to have a wider margin of leisure than many who live in more fully "developed" regions.

–Joseph Wood Krutch (1961)

... He was living his life and I was living mine. Fate and circumstances of our birth in countries where there were different economic standards had decreed that I should travel with trucks and canned goods, gasoline stoves, bacon, eggs, butter, and sugar. He was traveling on a burro with two pack burros, one of which carried a little barrel of water. He had his two dogs and he had their loyal friendship. In his way, he was as rich as I was, or perhaps richer, and any attempt to have sought his friendship on any other basis than mutual understanding and long acquaintances would have been an insult to his dignity.

And so I stood watching him going down the road, his burros shuffling along at a rapid walk, ears wiggling back and forth, and the two dogs trotting along at his side. I don't know what his thoughts were. I only know that he never once looked back.

–Erle Stanley Gardner (1947)

Rancho Santa Inés, Cataviña–

After a sumptuous dinner that could include quail, deer, carne asada or sea turtle—always with the Señoras famous enchiladas—we would share a campfire and music before turning in for the night. My fellow travelers were mostly truck drivers hauling live sea turtles north to Ensenada, trucks heavy with onyx from El Marmol, stake trucks loaded with cured hides, a Baja Buff or two, sometimes a prospector with his burro train, once in a while a goat herder and his charges going God-knows-where, or a scientist, such as a botanist doing field collecting. A real mixed bag sharing the courtyard, and sleeping under the stars.

–Marion Smothers (circa 1960s)

Palmer

Part of the magic is in the setting—one of the most picturesque deserts imaginable. Here, the Author of Nature has gathered her rarest of offspring—blue palms, cardóns, boojum and elephant trees—as if for a family portrait. Posing in stark relief are boulders of silver-flecked granite on a carpet of quartz sand.

At night the stars sparkle with incomparable brilliancy—unless there happens to be a full moon, as is the case tonight. In the reflected illumination one can easily read or go for a stroll, as I'm about to. The first-time visitor, off guard from the heat of the day, is sent bundling from an inexplicable arctic chill in the night.

Always a welcome sight for weary travelers is the Rancho, where time seems to stand still. Campers settle in along the wash while travelers with their own bedding can stay in one of the former bunkhouse rooms. What Rancho Santa Inés is mostly about, though, is dining. The scene is the same for dinner and breakfast: guests seated at a large outdoor table become instant friends over cervezas and the swapping of tall Baja tales. In the meantime, Matilda prepares some of the most savory Mexican dishes to be found up or down the peninsula, something she has been doing for thirty years.

–Gregory MacDonald (2001)

In Loreto, we trip and toil under nine grocery bags. The volume of Mexican music from passing cars shakes windows and rattles palm fronds. Loudspeakers on the roof of a battered Pinto endorse a new electorial candidate so loudly that we drop the bags and hold hands over our ears as it passes; people in street-side houses defend themselves by cranking up the volume of their televisions.

The first mission in Baja California, founded 296 years ago by Salvatierra, was rebuilt in 1704 on its present site. After a chubasco razed most of Loreto in 1829, sparing the church, the capitol was moved to La Paz. The church's square has been recobbled, although the boxy shape appears more jailhouse than church. A clock has been added to the highest turret. The antiqued church bell's pealing with no correlation to the clock or any religious event, almost drowns out the Pinto—prowling down the street.

In the same square where Father Salvatierra preached to the heathens—condemning pitaya revelries and wanton behavior—Loreto teens are sucking cherry Popsicles and shouting come-ons to would-be mates across the church plaza.

-Jonathan Waterman (1995)

Palmer

Strangely enough, the most amazing sight in connection with one's visit to Loreto is 22 miles from the old Ciudad Principal. Climbing steadily through a scenic narrow canyon with dense palm growth, one emerges before the Moorish stone church of San Javier, the most perfectly preserved and finest Jesuit church in Baja. Built 1774–1758, it is amazing for its design, embellishments and the shaping setting evidenced in its stonework. The altar mayor was brought from Mexico City in 32 boxes transported by mule-back and brigantine ...

The whole experience is the essence of incongruity and anachronism; San Javier is completely out of place and out of period. But the impressive edifice with baptistery, spiral staircase, choir loft, twin lateral chapels, bell tower and ornate golden reredos, before which the sanctuary lamp burns today as it has burned for over two hundred years, is perhaps a rare monument in a largely transitory world.

What a lesson in stone and guilt, sitting in an almost immemorial wasteland!

–Tadeo R. T. Brenton (1963)
(Found in *Baja California Yearbook for Las Californias Magazine.*)

Bahía de La Concepción, nearly landlocked and twenty-five miles long, is one of the most beautiful places on the gulf coast north of La Paz. Turquoise and ultramarine waters wash its precipitous shores with the milky blueness of tropical seas the world over ... There is contradiction; the harshness of the known immediate environment denies the agreeableness of the remote and unverifiable scene, denies its dreamlike unreality, and the feeling that one experience is truer than the other sets up a counterpoint that arouses a bewildered exaltation ...

Baja California is epitomized by this resplendent bay, where the real and the romantic are juxtaposed. Just as other opposites are up and down the lower and wilder California—the chill winds against the oppressive heat; torrents and mud against the dusty desiccation; forested shade against desert waste ... The very geology testifies to agony on a grand scale, when the granite spine and its metamorphic core, upheaved in eons past, was shattered by volcanic thrust and buried in the ensuing floods of lava.

–Eliot Porter (1967)

I couldn't help but think of the various conditions of the seas as different mood. I knew when the sea was angry and I knew when it was being coy. The sea played by its own rules, and to succeed Verlen and I had to accept them. I had not been able to change the sea one bit, but it was changing me.

My canoe was the part of me that belonged to the sea. The unique vehicle allowed me to move with the water, gliding in a continuous fluid breath. I wanted to believe that my canoe was an effective camouflage so that the sea would think me of its own, but the sea was not fooled. The wind came up and waves reared like a herd of broncos, kicking to buck us off the water before noon on January 26.

Verlen and I had made good progress; we had paddled 70 miles in 36 hours since leaving Santa Rosalia when we pulled ashore at Punta San Juan Bautista on a patch of sand beach.

The desert seems best suited to bite and prick and is not thought of as a friendly place, but throughout our journey the desert had offered us rest. The desert is a masterpiece of stillness, and it was that when we were being still that we best understood the definite progress our movement had brought.

–Valerie Fons (1982)

Palmer

The first of Concepcion Bay's superlatives is mere size, for it is some twenty-five miles across and that means nearly as big as our own San Francisco Bay proper. But it is also perfectly proportioned and in every respect designed as if for maximum beauty and impressiveness. The water could not be bluer, the great sandy beaches could not be whiter, and their curves could not be more exquisitely right.

The sky is almost as blue as the water and the few palms which here and there dot the open beaches are placed as though they had been put by design just where the eye finds them most effective. Herons, both white and great blue, stand motionless; the smooth, very deep water of the bay is broken by a surfacing whale; and in the chinks of the red volcanic cliffs, sometimes only a few hundred yards from the shore, grow great masses of a flame-colored, almost luminescent-seeming flower with shiny deep green leaves and blossoms that look as though made of lacquer.

–Joseph Wood Krutch (1961)

THE BAY OF CONCEPTION

Hot squalls of animation
Shores of blue and green.

Wake of sleek ponga
Streaming toward the fishing grounds
Flat sea sunrise.

Frigates are the gulls' companions
They are friends in need
And thieves in deed.

Pelicans dive
On blue currents
Where the fish collide
A feeding frenzy.

The old fishermen are singing
The nets are keening in the wind.

French angels ascend the coral reef
Courting the divers who descend.

The Spanish hogfish are skittish
My finger caresses the trigger.

–Ben Stoltzfus (2000)

Palmer

Nearby, other tropical species probed and tore and circled the coral—idols and surgeonfish, triggerfish with sloping foreheads and horselike incisors, and the damselfish, small but fiercely territorial. A snorkeler from Cuba or Jamaica might recognize a third or more of these species, which are twins, or analogs, to Caribbean species. Until two to five million years ago, the Sea of Cortez was distantly connected to the Caribbean by a natural rift through Central America—the Panama seaway. In the ages since the seaway closed, species on both sides have continued to evolve, making them distinct species ...

Tropical fish colors—turquoise, emerald, lemon yellow, stoplight red—drew me ever deeper, and made me forget, however briefly, about my own need to breathe. Some of the fish were flat and round like dinner plates, others were sleek and bullet-shaped. All wore the round-eyed, purse-lipped expression of the perpetually surprised.

–Andromeda Romano-Lax (2002)

The shore fishing in the tide pools around Puerto Chileno had us wondering if we were still on this planet. At Chileno a series of circular, oblong, and angular tidal basins begin in a shelf that stretches for miles along the shore line. In some of these pools the water is 40 feet deep. In the first pool we tried, fishes that appeared to be all colors of the rainbow floated up from a 5-fathom bottom, criss-crossed the 50-foot-wide pool, and glided in and out of small caves in the honeycombed wall. After I cast a lure down the full length and started to retrieve, a romping carnival of multicolored fishes swarmed out in pursuit of the lure. It seemed that every large crevice, crag, and tunnel was jammed with marine life.

Out came yard-long blue crevalle, lineal striped blue and gold snapper, red Colorado snapper, the curious Chinese-design chino mero, yellow striped goatfish, green and brown-spotted leopard grouper, brilliant golden grouper. There were orange-slashed triggerfish, turquoise-hued parrotfish, and a multitude of small wrasses glowing in unearthly radiance. In the words of Frank Dufresne, "It was like something swimming right out of a hophead's dream."

–Ray Cannon, *The Sea of Cortez* (1966)

Mulegé is an attractive oasis settlement two miles from the Gulf, on the Arroyo de Santa Rosalía. Dense groves of date palms make a welcome contrast to the surrounding barren country and give the impression of a tropical paradise such as one might expect to find in the South Seas. There is a pervasive atmosphere of ease and tranquility, perhaps due in part to the high occurrence of malaria among the inhabitants.

The town itself is on a slight elevation on the left bank of the arroyo, a neat compact group of low adobe houses centering on a tiny plaza. Below on all sides are small plots of irrigated land among the date palms, where many kinds of semi-tropical fruits and vegetables are grown.

Above the town is a large federal prison. The inmates are allowed considerable freedom and may work for wages anywhere in the town. Prisoners rarely want to escape from Mulegé.

The Jesuits founded the mission of Mulegé in 1705, on the site of an Indian ranchería called Caamanc-ca-galejá.

–Peter Gerhard and Howard Gulick (1962)

At the upper end of the village [Mulegé] are the ruins of the church and other buildings which the Jesuits founded here about the year 1770. These men must have been influenced by a strong zeal to have induced them to sacrifice the comforts and luxuries of Spain and Mexico and come to his desert and live for the benefit of a few scattered and miserable converts. The remains of their labours showed they were men of active enterprise; they reared such structures of stone in the desert. The little water and ground capable of cultivation; they appropriated the necessities for the sustenance of life. The gardens of the mission still contain the fig, the olive, the vine, the date, the orange, and the pomegranate in abundance. Each little spot of earth to which the water could be brought produces its rich harvest, but the Indian for whose benefit it is said these priests laboured—is no more to be seen in this native land. The oppression of those same priests in after years destroyed the race, and now it is a curiosity to see an Indian of the stock of those who were once the lords of the soil.

–James H. Bull (1843)

Baja California has places where man can let wilderness last if he elects to. They will help us to remember that man can never put the wilderness back. It doesn't work that way. Baja is a good place to respect what man discovers there and leaves alone, not what he brings there to change it, wherever he comes from. It is a place to learn. Without Baja's wildness, the world is just that much closer to becoming a cage.

–David Brower (1967)

We careen through the desert. The bus driver is reckless and the desert is green. Between the giant cardon cacti the flinty ground is covered with yellow flowers and thorn bushes delicately flecked with crimson. Guillermo Velasques is amazed. He points out the window. "This orange flower, this is malva. She comes with all the rain." Then he addresses the flowers themselves: "In thirteen years here I never see you! Nice to meet you!"

–Peter Heller (1992)

The desert was a giant flower show. After the heavy rains, the whole area burst with blossoms. It was, they told us, the greatest floral display the desert had ever put on, the spring after the rains forced us to turn back. Every plant bears flowers, and most of them fruit or edible seeds, or is useful in some way to man or beast.

–Pel Carter (1967)

The rough wheel-tracks into Baja's desert heartland open to the adventurous a wonderful variety of terrain, habitat, and view. One's eyes shift from boldly sweeping distance to rich roadside detail and back again.

The five-to-six-hundred mile Vizcaino-Magdalena segment of Baja's granite spine is ribbed and flanked with alluvial interior and sand-blown coastal valleys; outwash plains; ocean-facing lagoons, salt-pan, dunes, offshore islands; granite hills, volcanic mesas and plateaus, recent cinder cones and lava flows; rugged but not high mountain ridges; low playas, or dry lake beds; and a complex drainage pattern of barrancas, arroyos, large and small erosion channels, crosscutting the whole in every direction.

The Kaleidoscope of impressions—astonishment, delight, bewilderment, perhaps satiety near the end of a long, hot, dusty day, leaves the traveler with more questions than answers ...

Baja is still, as Joseph Wood Krutch said in *The Forgotten Peninsula*, "a land where new discoveries can be made." Anyone with open eyes and a little curiosity can play the discovery game.

–Don Greame Kelly (1971)

When you're off the pavement, you're in the realm of the Baja 1000 road race: no road signs, no road maintenance and sometimes no road at all. It's sand pits, sharp rocks, unbelievably steep grades, washouts, slides, teeth cracking ruts, blow-outs, breakdowns and uncertain supplies of gas, water, food, and beer.

–Carl Franz (1995)

Another thing you can do on washboard is try to "fly" it. Ernest Hemingway was one of the first to write about this technique during his African safaris. Basically, it means you try to accelerate your vehicle to a speed at which your tires touch only the tops of the washboard, giving you the wonderful illusion that you are driving on a smooth road.

Generally, this takes at least 30 m.p.h., depending on your vehicle, how deep the washboard is, etc. This is something like breaking the sound barrier, since there is a period of maximum vibration that must be overcome before things begin to smooth out. Not all washboard can be flown. Out on the rough stuff, the vibration is so severe you will destroy your vehicle and perhaps forget who you are before you can attain flight speed ...

Probably the most frustrating thing about driving on washboard is being left in a choking cloud of dust as the Mexicans pass you at 60 m.p.h. We still haven't figured out how they do this, but we think maybe it has something to do with the water.

–Neil Kelly and Gene Kira (1988)

The grandly named Camino Real, or King's Highway, that linked them [the missions] was named for a series of monarch's who didn't support the effort economically, later demanded a financial cut of what turned out to be nothing, and finally sabotaged the whole enterprise; the highway itself was never more than the frailest track, and those who seek it today are perhaps deceived by its name, or romanced by its obscurity.

–Bruce Berger (1998)

Fast car on the mesquite road
Racing the song of the cicadas.

The trail is a pale yellow ribbon
Waving toward the horizon.

Cholla ocotillo rabbit and sage
The coyote is hungry.

A desiccated cow
A gutted rusting chassis
Two carcasses.

Road sign: Curva Peligrosa
Beyond it glass shards
Sparkle like grass.

Crosses on the road mark a death
Empty tequilas mark the passage.

–Ben Stoltzfus (2000)

Palmer

That night I awakened about midnight and watched the stars, the palm fronds silhouetted against the sky, and listened to the sound of the water purling by my bed.

Here in this crystal-clear air there was enough starlight to distinguish patterns in cloth and make out the differences in color in the pattern.

A few hundred feet above me was a cave where whole civilizations had lived and loved, had laughed and died, and become dust. Here in this canyon there were things that had never been seen by modern eyes. We were a part of Baja California that up to this time had remained completely unknown. We were indeed in the hidden heart of the peninsula.

The blazing brilliance of the stars was uncanny. The overall silence was an impressive backdrop against the sound of the stream which had furnished life-giving water for thousands of years to people who had completely vanished from earth, leaving behind them only artifacts and a series of paintings executed by unknown artists ... Here was nature-nature in the raw, but kind, beneficial, healing nature.

–Erle Stanley Gardner (1962)

FIELD NOTEBOOK

(that which is intelligible.—ed.)

P. 5

Clams, crabs, oysters boiled in salt water

Indian hunters kill two deer
Carried seven miles
Shell ground to skin deer

Mesquite, ironwood, creosote, pitahay, saguaro, ocotillo

Barracade from wind by huge turtle shells

P. 6

Totoaba—big fish feed on small bones
Lashed by mesquite rope to raft
"Coe-Whem—Coyote Man"
Big Lizard

Lobster roasted on coals Soft musical lingo

Dedicated to my friend and companion Roberto Thompson
My friends the Seris
The Indians of Tiburon Island

–Edward Davis (1926)

COYOTE

Winds continued to signal a healthy windstorm
As we lay at anchor early one morn
In the darkness there came a familiar sound
The only one like it in Mexico I've found
A howling and yipping rode the wind to my ears
I hadn't heard that song for years
I listened to their progress as they crossed the sand
It was the Baja Coyote Traveling Band

–Janet Davis (1999)

Palmer

This is a country of baffling mirages. The air shimmers with the heat, and you travel in sort of a dream world between hallucination and reality. Ahead you see what appears to be a three-story house of strange conformation. It turns out to be a wrecked automobile at the side of the road. Off to the east you become aware, or you think you become aware, of the gulf; a long promontory with clumps of trees or shrubbery extends out into it, enclosing a bay on which there are boats, some with sails.

You are tempted to look for a turnoff, hoping for a place on the beach where you can rest and escape the terrible heat and glare of the desert. Your eyes search the roadside. When you raise them again the promontory is gone. The trees and boats, too. The horizon has changed utterly. Now there are four horizontal bands of color. Nearest is the monotonous tan of the desert; then a band of indigo blue; then finally the paler blue of the infinite sky.

But all of it is a little uncertain, dancing in the heat, and you wait for it, too, to disappear as had the promontory and the sailboats. But the colors are real. The dazzling white is the salt-caked coastal plain; the deep blue is really the gulf.

–William Weber Johnson (1972)

Palmer

We are under way Monday morning just after seven o'clock. Sancho is slow but sure footed and never stumbles. Mother and I take turns riding him ...

The desert is not at all what I thought it would be. I thought it would be just barren sand. It is not. The sand is mostly white, but there is a white grass and the golleto—or cracker grass—which grows in bunches and looks something like green oats. Then there is the grease wood brush, and the palo verde trees, and the thorny mesquite scrub trees, and the cardon—or tree cactus—and the barrel—or visuage—cactus which looks like a keg. The worst cactus is the cholla which is made up of joints armed with thorns ...

The prettiest cactus is the ocotillo, which is made up of a number or green poles coming out from a central spot and extending outward in swaying lengths. Now at the end each length there is a pretty red flower. Today we see twenty-five varieties of desert flowers. They are lovely. We see them in shades of purple and yellow and orange and red and pink, we see them white and blue. Mother and I pick little nosegays of them, and father spies out some and brings them to us.

–Mary North (1930)

The dipping, twisting branches of the Cirio make it the most unusual plant on the peninsula. Also called the "Boojum" tree after a character in Lewis Caroll's *The Hunting of the Snark*, the Cirio shows its most dramatic whimsy along this road. Cirio by the hundreds soar to the heavens, branch into grotesque fingers, return to earth in arches fit for a wedding ceremony.

If this plant could be described as lovely, it would be after a rain when it quickly dresses from tip to toe in a coat of bright green leaves which it sheds quickly to conserve moisture. The flowers in late spring and summer range from white to yellow. They often appear red, however, with a setting sun and could be mistaken for a flame at the top of the tapered candle.

–Patti and Tom Higginbotham (1996)

One finds the boojum wild only in Lower California. If I had not seen it with my own eyes, I should not believe it, for it is far more improbable looking as a tree than the giraffe is as an animal.

–Joseph Wood Krutch (1967)

There is an uneasy feeling of change and uncertainty—even danger—about the desert coast of the northern gulf. Twice each day huge tides race inland over the flats. Part of the sea water is lost to evaporation under the intense heat of the sun and the desert winds, and the flats are glazed with a blinding white rime of salt. The tides also constantly rearrange the shore, shifting mud and sand, polishing the stones, revising the shape of the headlands. This week's landmark may have disappeared by next week, or it may still be there in a wholly different and confusing guise.

–William Weber Johnson (1972)

It was almost midnight before we heard a low, distant moaning which we at once recognized, from the description given to us, as the burrow [tidal bore]. The moaning gradually increased to a roar which brought back to mind the equally alarming racket of a great herd of stampeding cattle. Then we were suddenly involved in chaos, with a maelstrom of swirling water all about us. Our snubbing device fortunately worked admirably, bringing our head round before we were capsized, and starting us fairly up the steep wave-front which suddenly appeared close aboard us. The drift-stump pulled loose from its muddy environment, before we could cast off from it, and thereafter served us as a drag as we were whirled away up river again, stern first, in the direction of Yuma.

–Godfrey Sykes (1895)

But though the Boulder Dam stopped the volume of water and its accompanying silt load, it did not halt the mighty tidal bore, or provide any guardian to take the place of the deposited silt load in halting the salt water in its rush up-stream. No longer checked by steadily renewed deposits of mud, the mountainous tide, hemmed in by the encroaching banks and funneled up by the sloping bottom of the gulf, hurled itself against the bed and banks of the river. Moving inland unopposed, it loosened silt deposits over a tremendous area. Then turning about and rushing seaward, it carried with it thousands of tons for which there were no longer any adequate replacements from the crests of the Rockies.

–Randolph Leigh (1940)

Palmer

The name Vagabundos is a title and a way of life that sea drifters apply to themselves. Their origin, according to one version, was with some Yaqui Indians around Bahia Adair in the north end of the Cortez who learned to use sailing canoes a century or so ago and deserted the land for a pleasanter life on the warm and abounding Sea. Happy-go-lucky Mexicans who disliked working for others and being subjected to rules and laws of the landside society irritated the Indians.

Since then they have been joined by an assortment of other men, from peons to college professors, who preferred complete freedom, breaking off land ties to follow a life without tensions or concerns.

The roaming vagabundos del mar, or sea gypsies, are not to be compared with vagrants, bindle stiffs, or drifters, for they ask favors of no man and a few women. Each has his own magic carpet—a weather-beaten canoe hewn from a single tree and propelled by a triangular sail or by oars that are seldom used. Usually, their only other earthly possessions are confined to heavy hand lines and hooks for fishing, an apron for spreading sharks, turtles, and fish, a bucket, a couple of pots for cooking, a machete, wine bottles for water, a blanket, and a coil of rope.

Store foods are generally limited to small supplies of beans, tortilla meal, dried chile peppers, and salt. Every few months, when additional supplies are needed, they take live turtles or salted shark meat to the nearest town for trading. Even in this contact they feel beholden only to the freely-giving sea. Their only conflicts are with the Sea's storms.

–Ray Cannon (1966)

It was learned that the entire Seri race [of Tiburon Island] does not number five hundred people and that they are rapidly decreasing in population. Unlike other Indian tribes the Seris have no connection in race, language or manners with any other Indians ...

Physically the Seris are tall, well formed and athletic. Intellectually they occupy the lowest position in the scale of humanity, excepting possibly that of some of the people of the polar regions. The Seris know nothing whatever about agriculture or mechanics. They use a reed raft for a boat and subsist principally upon turtle and fish food. It is claimed that the Seris frequently run down deer and other game, catching it with their hands, and that no other Indians are so fleet of foot ...

Contrary to the customs of other Indians, the Seris have no fixed habitations and do not continuously live in huts or houses. They sometimes shelter themselves in a reed shack, and during the rainy season some of these shacks are roofed with turtle shells ...

Compared to the average North American Indian, the Seris lack dignity of character, stolidity of manner and knowledge of what to do to live decently and comfortably. Should civilization ever bend its footsteps into the present Seri domain there soon would be either a few more good Indians in the happy hunting grounds or a sudden conversion of a set of worthless aborigines into better citizens.

–C. G. Conn (1908)

El día abre la mano
Tres nubes
Y estas pocas palabras

Al alba busca su nombre lo naciente
Sobre los troncos soñolientos centellea la luz
Galopan las montañas a la orilla del mar
El sol entra en las agues con espuelas
La piedra embiste y rompe claridades
El mar se obstina y crece al pie del horizonte
Tierra confusa imminencia de escultura
El mundo alza la frente aún desnuda
Piedra pulida y lisa para grabar un canto
La luz despliega su abanico de nombres
Hay un comienzo de himno como un árbol
Hay el viento y nombres hermosos en el viento

The hand of day opens
Three clouds
And these few words

At daybreak the newborn goes looking for a name
Upon the sleep-filled bodies the light glitters
The mountains gallop to the shore of the sea
The sun with his spurs on is entering the waves
Stony attack shattering clarities
The sea resists rearing to the horizon
Confusion of land imminence of sculpture
The naked forehead of the world is raised
Rock smoothed and polished to cut a poem on
Display of light that opens its fan of names
Here is the seed of a singing like a tree
Here are the wind and names beautiful in the wind

–Octavio Paz (1963)

Palmer

It has been more than just a physical adventure. Baja gave me an intermittent, fleeting glance into another world; not just a world of columned cacti and strange creatures, but a world of spiritual experience a thousand times more different from my old rational, logical, scientific conception of reality than the desert was from the greens and greys of England ...

Maybe the greatness of man lies in the fact that not only can he learn from the past but he can also learn from the future. And there lies my feeling of brotherhood. With the likes of Ugarte, Salvatierra, Steinbeck, Vizcaino and Erle Stanley Gardner. We were all drawn to Baja and in touch with each other, sharing a common sense of the sacred. As Steinbeck had said of the Gulf: "There is some quality that trips a trigger of recognition so that one finds oneself nodding and saying inwardly, 'Yes I know' and we know we must go back if we live, and don't know why." I belong to them; they belong to me. I lived in them. They live in me. And we all belong to Baja.

–Graham Mackintosh (1995)

Palmer

The shape of the trip was an integrated nucleus from which weak strings of thought stretched into every reasonable reality, and a reality which reached into us though our perceptive nerve trunks. The laws of thought seemed really one with the laws of things. There was some quality of music here, perhaps not to be communicated, but sounding clear in our minds ...

We liked it very much. The brown Indians and the gardens of the sea, and the beer and the work, they were all one thing and we were that one thing too.

–John Steinbeck (1940)

INDEX OF AUTHORS

INDEX OF IMAGES

ILLUSTRATIONS BY JUDITH PALMER

OTHER IMAGES

BIBLIOGRAPHY

WORKS CITED

Ascension, Father Antonio de la. *Vather Antonio de la Ascension's Account of the Voyage of Sebastian Viscaino*. Henry R. Wagner. *California Historical Society Quarterly*. April, 1928.

Baegert, Jakob. *Letter to Brother in Srassburg, 1752*. Berkeley: University of California Bancroft Library Microfilm.

Bancroft, Griffing. *The Flight of the Least Petrel*. New York: G. P. Putnam's Sons, 1932.

________. *The Song of Sonora*. Mariposa, California: Jerseydale Ranch Press, 1993.

Belden, L. Burr. *Baja California Overland*. Glendale, California: La Siesta Press, 1965.

Berger, Bruce. *Almost an Island*. Tucson: University of Arizona Press, 1998.

Bolton, Herbert Eugene. *Rim of Christendom—A Biography of Eusebio Francisco Kino*. Tucson: University of Arizona Press, 1984.

Botello, Judy Goldstein. *The Other Side: Journeys in Baja California*. Sunbelt Publications: San Diego, California 1998.

Brenton, Tadeo (ed.) *Baja California Yearbook of Las Californias Magazine*, 1963.

Brower, David. *Baja California and the Geography of Hope*. Sierra Club and Ballentine Books, 1969.

Browne, J. Ross. "Explorations in Lower California, 1886-87." *Harper's New Monthly Magazine*, August–October 1868.

Bryant, Walter F. "The Cape Region of Baja California." *Zoe 2* (1891): 185–201.

Bull, James H. 1843. Reference not available.

Cahill, Tim. "Good Clean Fun in Baja." *Outside Magazine*, January 1993: 72–78.

Cannon, Ray. *The Sea of Cortez*. Menlo Park, California: Lane Publishing, 1966.

Carter, Pel. *Trails and Tales of Baja*. Lake San Marcos, California: Southwest Arts Foundation, 1967.

Castaneda, Pedro de. In Charles Chapman, *A History of California—The Spanish Period*. New York: MacMillan, 1921.

Clavigero, Don Francisco Javier. *The History of* [Lower] *California*. Translation by Lake and Gray. Riverside, California: Manessier Publishing Company, (reprint) 1937.

Conn, C. G. *The Cruise of the Comfort*. Elkhart, Indiana: Truth Publishing Co, 1908.

Cooke, Captain Edward. *A Voyage to the South Sea and Round the World*. London: Lintot and Gosling, 1712.

Cortés, Hernán. Fourth Letter to the King. In Charles Chapman, *A History of California—The Spanish Period*. New York: MacMillan, 1921.

Crosby, Harry. *Antigua California*. Albuquerque: University of New Mexico Press, 1994.

________. *The Cave Paintings of Baja California*. San Diego: The Copley Press, 1975.

Davis, Edward G. *The Edward H. Davis Papers. Field Notebook #13*. March, 1926. Microfilm holding, San Diego Historical Society.

Davis, Janet. *Sea of Cortez Review*. San Diego: Sunbelt Publications, 1999.

Dunne, Peter Masten. *Black Robes in California*. San Francisco: University of San Francisco Press, 1966.

Eyles, Carlos. *The Last of the Blue Water Hunters*. Sand Diego, California: Watersport Publishing. 1991.

Fierro Blanco, Antonio de. *The Journey of the Flame*. New York: The Literary Guild, 1933.

Foerster, Leland. *The Californios*. Oceanside, California: Golden Raintree Press,

2003.
Fons, Valerie. *Keep it Moving—Baja by Canoe*. Seattle: The Mountaineers, 1986.
Franz, Carl. *The People's Guide to Mexico*. Santa Fe: John Muir Publications, Publications, 1995.
Gardner, Erle Stanley. *Land of Shorter Shadows*. New York: Morrow, 1948.
Gerhard, Peter and Howard Gulick. *Lower California Guidebook*. Glendale, California: The Arthur H. Clark Company, 1962.
Guzman, Nuno de. "Letter to the King of Spain, 1530." In Charles Chapman, *A History of California—The Spanish Period*. New York: MacMillan, 1921.
Hale, Howard. *Long Walk to Mulegé*. Kansas City: Pinkerton Publishing Co., 1980.
Hanna, Phil Townsend. "Some Other Americans." Article in Automobile Club of Southern California Magazine, *Touring Topics*, October–November, 1928.
Hardy, Robert William Hale. *Travels in the Interior of Mexico*. London: Bentley, 1829.
Heller, Peter. "Wild Baja." From *Buzzworm: The Earth Journal*. September–October, 1992.
Higginbotham, Patti and Tom. *Backroad Baja* (Central Region). San Diego: Sunbelt Publications, 1996.
Hilton, John W. *Sonora Sketch Book*. New York: MacMillan, 1947. (Two copies.)
________. *Hardly Any Fences*. Los Angeles: Dawson's Book Shop, 1977.
Hornaday, William T. *Campfires on Desert and Lava*. New York: Scribner, 1909.
Janes, John F. *The Adventures of Stickeen in Lower California (1874)*. Los Angeles: Dawson's Book Shop, 1972.
Johnson, William Weber. *Baja California*. Time-Life Books, 1972.
Kelly, Neil and Gene Kira. *The Baja Catch*. Valley Center, California: Apples and Oranges Publishing, 1997.
Kira, Gene. *King of the Moon—A Novel of Baja California*. Valley Center, California: Apples and Oranges Publishing, 1997.
Krutch, Joseph Wood. *The Forgotten Peninsula*. Tucson: University of Arizona Press, 1986.
________ with Photographs by Eliot Porter. *Baja California and the Geography of Hope*. San Francisco: The Sierra Club, 1967.
Lamb, Dana. *Enchanted Vagabonds*. New York: Harper, 1938.

Landauer, Lyndall Baker. *Scammon—Beyond the Lagoon*. Pasadena, California: Flying Cloud Press, 1986.

Leigh, Randolph. *Forgotten Waters*. Philadelphia: Lippincott, 1941.

Lewis, Leland R. *Baja Sea Guide. Vol. II*. San Franciso: Miller Freeman Publications, 1971.

Linck, Wenceslaus. *Wenceslaus Linck's Diary of His 1776 Expedition to Northern Baja California*. Trans. and ed. Ernest J. Burrus. Los Angeles: Dawson's Book Shop, 1966.

Mackintosh, Graham. *Into a Desert Place*. Idyllwild, California: Graham Mackinstosh, 1990.

________. *Journey With a Baja Burro*. San Diego: Sunbelt Publications, 2001.

Madin, Kent. "Whale Watching in Mag Bay Remembered." *Adventure Magazine*, Winter/Spring, 1994.

Martinez, Pablo. *A History of Lower California*. Mexico City: Martinez, 1961.

McDonald, Marquis. *Baja, Land of Lost Missions*. San Antonio, Texas: The Naylor Company, 1968.

McMahan, Mike. *There It Is: Baja!* Los Angeles: Mike McMahan, 1973.

________. *Adventures in Baja*. Los Angeles: McMahan, 1984.

Miller, Max. *Land Where Time Stands Still*. New York: Dodd, Mead, 1944. (Two copies.)

________. *The Cruise of the Cow*. New York: E. P. Dutton, 1951. (Two copies.)

Murray, Spencer and Ralph Poole. *Cruising the Sea of Cortez*. Palm Desert, California: Desert-Southwest, Inc., 1963.

North, Arthur Waldridge. *Camp and Camino in Lower California*. New York: Baker and Taylor, 1910. (two copies.)

________. *The Mother of California*. San Francisco: Paul Elder and Company, 1908.

North, Mary Ramsen. *Down the Colorado—by a Lone Girl Scout*. New York: Putnam, 1930.

Patchen, Marvin and Aletha. *Baja Adventures by Land, Air, and Sea*. Huntington Beach, California: Baja Trail Publications, 1981.

Paz, Octavio. *Early Poems, 1935–1955*. Trans. Muriel Rukeyser. New York: New Directions, 1963.

Peacock, Doug and Terrence Moore. *Baja!* New York: Little, Brown. First edition, 1991.

_______. *Baja Outpost*. San Diego: Sunbelt Publications, 2003.

Peterson,Walt. *The Baja Adventure Book*. Berkeley: Wilderness Press, 1998.

Polzer, Charles, S.J. *Kino—A Legacy*. Tucson: Jesuit Fathers of Southern Arizona, 1998.

Porter, Eliot and Joseph Wood Krutch. *Baja California and the Geography of Hope*. San Francisco: Sierra Club, 1967.

Quinn, Vernon. *Beautiful Mexico*. New York: Grosset and Dunlap, 1938.

Redmond, Jennifer. *Sea of Cortez Review*. San Diego: Sunbelt Publications, 1999.

Rizzoli. *Baja California*. New York: Rizzoli International Publications, 1987.

Romano-Lax, Andromeda. *Searching for Steinbeck's Sea of Cortez*. Seattle: Sasquatch Books, 2002.

Scammon, Captain Charles, 1856. In Krutch, *The Forgotten Peninsula*.

Schwartz, Elizabeth Maul. "Sea of Cortez." http://jinxschwartzcom.ipage.com/seaofcortez/seaofcortez.htm (accessed February, 1 2019).

Scott, Annette. *Cruising and Sketching Baja*. Flagstaff, Arizona: Northland Press, 1974.

Smith, W.C.S. "A Forty-Niner in Lower California." In Robert Cleland, *A History Of California: The American Period*. New York: MacMillan, 1922.

Smothers, Marion. *Vintage Baja*. Campo, California: One EAR Publications, 1993.

Steinbeck, John. *The Log From the Sea of Cortez*. New York: Viking/Penguin, 1951. (Two Copies.)

_______. *Sea of Cortez: A Leisurely Journal of Travel and Research*. New York: Penguin, 2009 (reprint from 1941 original).

Stoltzfus, Ben, and Judith Palmer. *The Puma Drinks the New Moon*. Talent, Oregon: Talent House Press, 2000.

Sykes, Godfrey. *A Westerly Trend*. Tucson: University of Arizona Press, 1972.

Taraval, Father Sigismundo. *Indian Uprisings in Lower California*. Trans. Marguerite Wilbur. Quevira Society, 1931.

Timberman, O. W. *Mexico's "Diamond in the Rough."* Los Angeles: Westernlore Press, 1959.

Venegas, Padre Miguel. *Empressas Apostólicas*. Manuscript, 1739. In Pablo Martinez, *A History of Lower California*. Mexico City: Pablo Martinez, 1960.

Viosca, Sebastian. *In the Peninsular Missions, 1808-1880*. Hong Kong: Libra Press, 1979.

Vosnesensii, J. G. *Aboard the Noslednik Aleksandra, 1842*. In Ann Zwinger, *A Desert Country Near the Sea*. New York: Harper and Row, 1983.

Waterman, Jonathan. *Kayaking the Vermilion Sea*. New York: Simon and Schuster, 1995.

Weber, Msgr. Francis J. *Fray Junipero Serra*. San Luis Obispo, California: EZ Nature Books, 1988.

Xantus, John. *Letters From North America, 1859*. Trans. Theodore and Helen Schoenman. Detroit: Waine State UP, 1975.

Zwinger, Ann. *A Desert Country Near the Sea*. New York: Harper & Row, 1983.

WORKS CONSULTED

Atkinson, Fred W. *The Argonauts of 1769*. Watsonville, California: Pajaronian Press, 1936.

Baxley, Robert. *A Miscellaneous Lawyer*. San Diego: Robert C. Baxley Books, 1999.

Bruns, Rebecca et al. *Hidden Mexico—Adventurer's Guide to the Beaches and Coasts*. Berkeley, California: Ulysses Press, 1989.

Billings, Frederick. *Letters from Mexico, 1859*. Woodstock, Vermont: The Elm Tree Press, 1936.

Braasch, Barbara (ed.) *Sunset Travel Guide to Mexico*. Menlo Park, California: Lane Publishing Company, 1982.

Bush, Wesley A. *Paradise to Leeward—Cruising the West Coast of Mexico*. Toronto: D. Van Nostrand Company, 1954.

Callcott, Wilfrid Hardy. *Church and State in Mexico*. Durham, North Carolina: Duke University Press, 1926.

Cannon, Ray. *How to Fish the Pacific Coast*. Menlo Park, California: Lane Publishing, 1954.

Case, Ted J. and Martin Cody. *Island Biogeography in the Sea of Cortés*. Berkeley, California: University of California Press, 1983.

Castañeda, Pedro de. *The Journey of Coronado*. Toronto: General Publishing,

1990.

Church, Mike and Terri. *Camping Mexico's Baja*. Kirkland, Washington: Rolling Homes Press, 2001.

Covey, Cyclone (trans. and ed.) *Adventures in the Unknown Interior of America*. Albuquerque: University of New Mexico Press, 1961.

Cummings, Joe. *Baja Handbook*. Chico, California: Moon Publications, 1992.

De Barco, Miguel. *Ethnology and Linguistics of Baja California*. Los Angeles: Dawson's Book Shop, 1981.

DeNevi, Don and Noel Francis Moholy. *Junípero Serra*. San Francisco: Harper & Row, 1985.

Dunaway, Philip and Mel Evans (eds.) *A Treasury of the World's Great Diaries*. Garden City, New York: Doubleday & Company, 1957.

Engstrand, Iris Wilson. *Joaquin Velazquez De Leon—Royal Officer in Baja California 1768-1770*. Los Angeles: Dawson's Book Shop, 1976.

Fowler, Gene. *Goodnight Sweet Prince: The Life and Times of John Barrymore*. New York: Viking, 1944.

Francez, Padre James Donald. *The Lost Treasures of Baja California*. Chula Vista, California: Black Forest Press, 1996.

French, Mary M. Billings. (ed.) *Letters From Mexico, 1859*. Woodstock, Vermont: The Elm Tree Press, 1936.

Garcia, Brenda. (ed.) *Baja Traveler*. Long Beach, California: Airguide Publications, 1988.

Gardner, Erle Stanley. *Hunting the Desert Whale*. New York: Morrow, 1960.

________. *Hovering Over Baja*. New York: Morrow, 1960.

________. *The Hidden Heart of Baja*. New York: Morrow, 1964.

________. *Off the Beaten Track In Baja*. New York: Morrow, 1961.

Garrison, Chuck. *Offshore Fishing—Southern California and Baja*. Los Angeles: Chuck Garrison, 1981.

Geiger, Maynard. *The Life and Times of Fray Junípero Serra*. Washington D. C.: Academy of American Franciscan History, 1959. (Two copies.)

Gerson, Noel B. *Sad Swashbuckler*. New York: Thomas Nelson, Inc., 1976.

Gibson, Charles. *Spain in America*. New York: Harper and Row, 1966.

Griffith, James S. *Beliefs and Holy Places*. Tucson: University of Arizona Press, 1992.

Guimont-Marceau, Stéphane. *Los Cabos and La Paz*. Toronto: Ulysses Travel

Publications, 2000.
Hager, Anna Marie (ed.) *The Filibusters of 1890*. Los Angeles: Dawson's Book Shop, 1968.
Haslip, Joan. *The Crown of Mexico*. New York: Holt, Rinehart and Winston, 1971.
Hodge, Frederick et al, (eds.) *Spanish Explorers in the Southern United States*. New York: Scribner, 1907.
Hulse, J. E. *Railroads and Revolutions–The Story of Roy Hoard*. El Paso: Managan Books, 1986.
Jones, Oakah L. *The Spanish Borderlands*. Los Angeles: Lorrin L. Morrison, 1974.
Jones, Vern. *Baja California Cruising Notes*. Julian, California: Seebreez Publications, 1976.
Johnson, Markes. *Discovering the Geology of Baja California*. Tucson: University of Arizona Press, 2002.
Johnson, William Weber et al. *Baja California*. Life Books, 1972.
Kelley, Don Greame. *Edge of a Continent*. New York: Galahad Book, 1972.
Kelsey, Harry. *Juan Rodríquez Cabrillo*. San Marino, California: Huntington Library Press, 1998.
Klink, Jerry. *The Mighty Cortez Fish Trap*. New York: Barnes & Co., 1974.
Kira, Gene S. *The Unforgettable Sea of Cortez—Baja California's Golden Age 1947–1977—The Life and Writings of Ray Cannon*. Cortez Publications.
Kulbach, Rod. *Baja Dreaming*. Friday Harbor, Washington: Fantasie Publishing, 2009.
Lindblad, Lisa and Sven-Olof (eds.) *Baja California*. New York: Rizzoli, 1987.
Lingenfelter, Richard. *The Rush of '89—The Baja California Gold Fever*. Los Angeles: Dawson's Book Shop, 1967.
MacDonald, Gregory. *The Baja Experience—Five Centuries of Adventure in Baja, California and the Sea of Cortez*. Fallbrook, California: MacDonald, 2006. UCSD Mandeville Collection.
________. Illustrated by Judith Palmer. *Isle of the Amazons in the Vermilion Sea*. Fallbrook, California: MacDonald and Palmer, revised 2011. UCSD Mandeville Collection.
________. Photograph collection, *Photographs, Baja California and Sonora, Mexico*. Fallbrook, California: MacDonald, 2006. UCSD Mandeville Collection.
________. *A Baby Flyer and the "Hansen Sea Cow."* San Jose: San Jose State

University Press: Steinbeck Studies, Vol. 16, 2005.
_______. *Rocks and Thorns—On the Trail with Padres Kino, Ugarte, and Serra in Lower California*. Fallbrook, California: MacDonald, 2011.
_______. *The North Family and the Lower California Effect*. Riverside, California: MacDonald, 2014.
MacLachlan, Colin M. *The Forging of the Cosmic Race—A Reinterpretation of Colonial Mexico*. Berkeley: University of California Press,1980.
Mathes, W. Michael (trans and ed.). *First from the Gulf to the Pacific*. Los Angeles: Dawson's Book Shop. 1969.
_______. *The Conquistador in California—The Voyage of Fernando Cortés to Baja California in Chronicles and Documents*. Los Angeles: Dawson's Book Shop, 1973.
_______. *The Pearl Hunters in the Gulf of California 1668*. Los Angeles: Dawson's Book Shop, 1974.
_______. *Clemente Guollén—Explorer of the South*. Los Angeles: Dawson's Book Shop, 1979.
Mayo, C. M. *Miraculous Air—Journey of a Thousand Miles through Baja California, the Other Mexico*. Minneapolis: Milkweed Editions, 2002.
Meyer, Michael et al. *The Course of Mexican History*. New York: Oxford University Press, 1999.
Miller, Kristine et al. *Mexico's Baja California*. Costa Mesa, California: The Automobile Club of Southern California, 2004.
Miller, Tom. *Angler's Guide to Baja California*. Huntington Beach, California: Baja Trail Publications, 1979.
_______. *Eating Your Way Through Baja*. Huntington Beach, California: Baja Trail Publications, 1986.
Moss, Jackie. *Baja Traveler*. Long Beach, California: Airguide Publications, 1974.
Niemann, Greg. *Baja Legends*. San Diego: Sunbelt Publications, 2002.
Nunis, Doyce B. (ed.) *Journey of James H. Bull Baja California 1843–45*. Los Angeles: Dawson's Book Shop, 1965.
Officer, James. *The Pimería Alta*. Tucson: The Southwestern Mission Research Center, 1996.
Older, Mrs. Fremont. *California Missions*. New York: Tudor Publishing, 1945.
O'Reilly, James and Larry Habegger (eds.) *Travelers' Tales Mexico*. Berkeley: Publishers Group West, 2001. (Two copies.)

Pan America Union. *Motoring in Mexico*. Washington D.C.: General Secretariat, 1958.

Paz, Octavio. Early Poems *1935–55*. Bloomington, Indiana: Indiana University Press, 1963.

Pepper, Choral. *Baja California*. Pasadena, California: Ward Ritchie Press, 1975.

Polzer, Charles. *A Kino Guide—His Missions–His Monuments*. Tucson: Southwestern Mission Research Center, 1976.

Potter, Ginger. *Baja Book IV*. El Cajon, California: Baja Source, 1996.

Pourade, Richard F. *Time of the Bells*. San Diego: The Union-Tribune Publishing Company, 1961. (two copies.)

________. *The Call to California*. San Diego: The Union-Tribune Publishing Company,1968.

Prescott, William. *History of the Conquest of Mexico*. New York: The Modern Library, 1967.

Redmond, Jennifer. *Sea of Cortez Review 1999–2001*. San Diego: Sunbelt Publications, 1999–2001.

Salazar, Ruben. *Border Correspondent*. Berkeley: University of California Press, 1998.

Sanford, Paul. *Where the West Never Died*. San Antonio: The Naylor Company, 1968.

Senterfitt, Arnold D. *Airports of Baja California*. Vista, California: Baja Bush Pilots, 1989.

Schulte-Peevers, Andrea et al. *Baja California*. Oakland: Lonely Planet Publications, 2003.

Simon, Kate. *Mexico—Places and Pleasures*. New York: Crowell, 1979.

Smith, Fay Jackson. *Father Kino in Arizona*. Phoenix: Arizona Historical Foundation, 1966.

Smith, Jack. *God and Mr. Gomez*. New York: Reader's Digest Press, 1974.

Smothers, Marion. *Vintage Baja—Adventures of a Gringa in Lower California*. Campo, California: In One Ear Publications, 1993.

Sommers, Jim. "In Search of Senor Big." *Rodde's Scuba Diving*, February 1994.

Southwest Museum. "Padre Kino—Depicted in Drawings by DeGrazia." Los Angeles: Southwest Museum, 1962.

Stanton, Larry. *Glory Days of Baja*. Camden, South Carolina: John Culler and Sons, 1996.

Strode, Hudson. *Timeless Mexico*. New York: Harcourt, Brace, 1944.

Sunset editorial staff. *Sunset Travel Guide to Baja California*. Menlo Park, California: Lane Publishing, 1971.

Swaim, Bernie. *Mi Baja, No Hurry No Worry*. Santee, California: Caballero Publishing, 2002.

Taylor, Lawrence and Maeve Hickey. *The Road to Mexico*. Tucson: University of Arizona Press,1997.

United States Navy Department. *Sailing Directions for the West Coast of Mexico*. Washington, DC: United States Government Printing Office, 1937.

Utley, Robert. *Changing Course—The International Boundary United States and Mexico, 1848–1963*. Tucson, Arizona: Southwest Parks and Monuments Association, 1996.

Weber, Msgr. Francis J. *The Peninsular California Missions 1808-1880*. Los Angeles: Dawson's Book Shop, 1979.

Wheelock, Walt. *Beaches of Baja*. Glendale, California: La Siesta Press, 1968.

Wilbur, Marguerite Eyer (ed.) *The Indian Uprising in Lower California, 1734–1737*. Los Angeles: The Quivira Society, 1931.

________. *Beaches of Sonora*. Glendale, California: La Siesta Press, 1972.

Williams, Jack. *Mexico's Baja California*. Sausalito, California: H. J. Williams, 1988.

ABOUT THE ILLUSTRATOR

JUDITH PALMER is a printmaker whose work is in the tradition of Jasper Johns, Cy Twombly, and Richard Diebenkorn. She explores the language of art and the process by which art's sign-system communicates its message-line, texture, color, and image. Palmer collects "found language"—numerals, words, sentences—from streets, walls, or waste paper, transfers their photo images onto zinc plates, and combines these elements with traditional, more rigid patterns and techniques of etching. The result is a dialectic: a movement back and forth between spontaneously flowing arabesques—that represent energy, aggression, and rebellion—and the rigid, straight lines of confinement and restriction. This combined language of spontaneity and restraint generates movement and tension between the different parts—form becomes content. Palmer's art is housed in the permanent collections of galleries and museums in Santa Monica, California; Knoxville, Tennessee; Riverside, California; and Pomona, California. She has received many awards, including the Margaret R. Hanenberg Award from the University of California, Riverside; the "Ink and Clay" Purchase Prize Award from California State Polytechnic in Pomona, California; and the "Jurors' Award" at the Pacific States Print Exhibition. Her line drawings for this volume are a departure from her more stylized, post-modern work.

ABOUT THE NARRATOR

Gregory MacDonald was the former Business and Facilities Administrator for the City of Riverside Public Library and the Riverside County Public Library System, a John Steinbeck scholar, and a Baja California enthusiast. He combined a passion for motorcycles with a fascination for Baja, its history, and its people. As an avid student of the exploration of Baja by the Spaniards and Mexicans, modern-day sailors, and adventurers, MacDonald, too, traveled deep into the mountains to visit isolated missions, towns, and farms. In the early 1970s, prior to the completion of Federal Highway 1 in 1975, he rode the thousand-mile length of the peninsula, alone, on his motorcycle, mostly off road. Later, he and his dog, Maggie, traveled around the United States in a rig exactly like John Steinbeck's, following the itinerary of the author's *Travels With Charlie*. MacDonald maintained an extensive library on Baja and documented his own travels with photographs and essays, including a land-based version of the voyage Steinbeck chronicled in *The Log from the Sea of Cortez*. In Cabo Pulmo, on the East Cape, he used an outboard motor—a Johnson Sea Horse—identical to the one that bedeviled Steinbeck, which the latter dubbed "Sea Cow" for its low power and lack of reliability. Gregory MacDonald was raised in Riverside, California, where he lived with his wife, Virginia, and his son, Matthew, who both are deceased. MacDonald passed away in 2015.

www.ingramcontent.com/pod-product-compliance
Lightning Source LLC
Chambersburg PA
CBHW041610260326
41914CB00012B/1448

* 9 7 8 1 9 4 6 3 5 8 1 4 1 *